Hidden in Plain Sight

Growing Your Business Abundantly One Overlooked Strategy at a Time

by George Zetts

COPYRIGHT AND DISCLAIMER

George Zetts

Published by:
Leader Publishing Worldwide
19 Axford Bay
Port Moody, BC V3H 3R4
Tel: 1 888 294 9151
Fax: 1 877 575 9151
Website: www.noresults-nofee.com

DEDICATION

I dedicate this book to Jesus. Thank you for your love and for giving me an abundant life.

To my wife Nicole – Thank you for your love and support. Thank you for reminding me that I have a voice that others need to hear and for encouraging me to fulfill my desire to help others live for more.

To my children:

Giorgio...you are a great big brother and protector.

Vincenzo...my Heart Warrior. You have a gentle spirit but are tougher than nails.

The Twins...I can't wait to meet you both!

Remember kids, you were made for greatness!

Finally, to all the business men and women out there adding value to the world. I am honored to do my part in helping you realize all of your hopes and dreams. Please don't settle for less when you know you were created for more!

CONTENTS

INTRODUCTION

Like many, I am a BIG fan of the TV Show *Seinfeld.* Many shows have come and gone but to me none have dethroned *Seinfeld* as the best of all time. There are so many notable scenes, plots and storylines that most of us can relate to. There is one episode in particular that embodies this book and your current business situation.

The Gymnast episode sees Kramer and the others mesmerized by one of those 3D art posters that were all the rage in the 90s. You may remember them – they were the ones that at first glance were an arbitrary design of shapes and color but once you looked at it the right way it revealed the hidden picture that was there all along. This is the story of your business.

At first glance, your business is what it is; an arbitrary combination of tactics that have created your current results. But look again. There is more. Actually, a lot more is possible. The good news is you don't need a Harvard MBA or to have some remarkable business mind to grow your business. You just need to know what to look for and this book will show just that. In fact, the legendary business and marketing genius Dan Kennedy says, "Most secrets are visible." Some of those "secrets" to your business success are within the pages of this book.

The keys to abundant business growth are in your possession. These strategies have worked for others and they can work for you as well. You have seen some, maybe even tried others but you will get a fresh look at them all in this book. Open your eyes to the possibilities and focus on what you have overlooked. And just like that 3D poster, the full potential of your business that has *Hidden in Plain Sight* will reveal itself to you!

1

Define Your Target Market

What is a Target Market?

Many businesses can't answer the question: *Who is your target market?* They have often made the fatal assumption that *everyone* will want to purchase their product or service with the right marketing strategy.

A target market is simply the group of customers or clients who will purchase a specific product or service. This group of people all have something in common, often age, gender, hobbies, or location.

Your target market, then, are the people who will buy your offering. This includes both existing and potential customers, all of whom are motivated to do one of three things:

- Fulfill a need
- Solve a problem
- Satisfy a desire

To build, maintain, and grow your business, you need to know who your customers are, what they do, what they like, and why they would buy your product or service. Getting this wrong – or not taking the time to get it

3

right – will cost you time, money, and potentially the success of your business.

The Importance of Knowing Your Target Market

Knowledge and understanding of your target market is the keystone in the arch of your business. Without it, your product or service positioning, pricing, marketing strategy, and eventually, your business could very quickly fall apart.

If you don't intimately know your target market, you run the risk of making mistakes when it comes to establishing pricing, product mix, or service packages. Your marketing strategy will lack direction, and produce mediocre results at best. Even if your marketing message and unique selling proposition (USP) are clear, and your brochure is perfectly designed, it means nothing unless it arrives in the hands (or ears) of the right people.

Determining your target market takes time and careful diligence. While it often starts with a best guess, assumptions cannot be relied on and research is required to confirm original ideas. Your target market is not always your ideal market.

Once you build an understanding of who your target market is, keep up with your market research. Having your finger on the pulse of their motivations and drivers – which naturally change – will help you to anticipate needs or wants and evolve your business.

Types of Markets

Consumer

The Consumer Market includes those general consumers who buy products and services for personal use, or for use by family and friends. This is the market category you or I fall into when we're shopping for groceries or clothes, seeing a movie in the theatre, or going out for lunch. Retailers focus on this market category when marketing their goods or services.

Institutional

The Institutional Market serves society and provides products or services for the benefit of society. This includes hospitals, non-profit organizations, government organizations, schools and universities. Members of the Institutional Market purchase products to use in the provision of services to people in their care.

Business to Business (B2B)

The B2B Market is just what it seems to be: businesses that purchase the products and services of other business to run their operations. These purchases can include products that are used to manufacture other products (raw or technical), products that are needed for daily operations (such as office supplies), or services (such as accounting, shredding, and legal).

Reseller

This market can also be called the "Intermediary Market" because it consists of businesses that act as channels for goods and services between other markets. Goods are purchased and sold for a profit – without any alterations. Members of this market include wholesalers, retailers, resellers, and distributors.

Determining Your Target Market

Product / Service Investigation

The process for determining your target market starts by examining exactly what your offering is, and what the average customer's motivation for purchasing it is. Start by answering the following questions:

Does your offering meet a basic need?	
Does your offering serve a particular want?	
Does your offering fulfill a desire?	
What is the lifecycle of your product / service?	
What is the availability of your offering?	

What is the cost of the average customer's purchase?	
What is the lifecycle of your offering?	
How many times or how often will customers purchase your offering?	
Do you foresee any upcoming changes in your industry or region that may affect the sale of your offering (positive/negative)?	

Market Investigation

- **On the ground.** Spend some time on the ground researching who your target market might be. If you're thinking about opening a coffee shop, hang out in the neighborhood at different times of the day to get a sense of the people who live, work, and play in the neighborhood. Notice their age, gender, clothing, and any other indications of income and activities.

- **At the competition.** Who is your direct competitor targeting? Is there a small niche that is being missed? Observing the clientele of your competition can help to build understanding of your target market, regardless of whether it is the same or opposite. For example, if you own a children's clothing boutique and the majority of middle-class mothers shop at the local department store, you may wish to focus on higher-income families as your target market.

- **Online.** Many cities and towns – or at least regions – have demographic information available online. Research the ages, incomes, occupations, and other key pieces of information about the people who live in the area you operate your business. From this data, you will gain an understanding of the size of your total potential market.

- **With existing customers.** Talk to your existing customers through focus groups or surveys. This is a great way to gather demographic and behavioral information, as well as genuine feedback about product or service quality and other information that will be useful in a business or marketing strategy.

Who is Your Market?

Based on your product / service and market investigations, you will be able to piece together a basic picture of your target market, and some of their general characteristics. Record some notes here. At this point, you may wish to be as specific as possible, or maintain some generalities. You can further segment your market in the next section.

Consumer Target Market Framework

Market Type:	Consumer	
Gender:	☐ Male	☐ Female
Age Range:		
Purchase Motivation:	☐ Meet a Need ☐ Serve a Want ☐ Fulfill a Desire	
Activities:		
Income Range:		
Marital Status:		
Location:	☐ Neighborhood ☐ City ☐ Region ☐ Country	
Other Notes:		

Institutional Target Market Framework

Market Type:	Institutional	
Institution Type:	☐ Hospital ☐ Non-profit ☐ School ☐ University ☐ Charity ☐ Government ☐ Church	
Purchase Motivation:	☐ Operational Need ☐ Client Want ☐ Client Desire	
Purpose of Institution:		
Institution's Client Base:		
Size:		
Location:	☐ Neighborhood ☐ City ☐ Region ☐ Country	
Other Notes:		

To learn how to avoid the 3 key mistakes all small business owners make, visit
www.AbundantGrowthStrategies.com

B2B Target Market Framework

Market Type:	Business to Business (B2B)
Company Size:	
Number of Employees:	
Purchase Motivation:	☐ Operations Need ☐ Strategy ☐ Functionality
Annual Revenue:	
Industry:	
Location(s):	
Purpose of Business:	
People, Culture & Values:	
Other Notes:	

Reseller Target Market Framework

Market Type:	Reseller
Industry:	
Client Base:	
Purchase Motivation:	☐ Operations Need ☐ Client Wants ☐ Functionality
Annual Revenue:	
Age:	
Location:	☐ Neighborhood ☐ City ☐ Region ☐ Country
Other Notes:	

Your Target Market: Putting It Together

Based on the information you gather from your product / service and market investigations, you should have a clear vision of your realistic target market. Here are a few examples of how this information is put together and conclusions are drawn:

Target Market Sample 1: Consumer Market

Business: Baby Clothing Boutique	**Business Purpose:**
Market Type: Consumer	*Meet a need* (provide clothing for infants and children aged 0 to 5 years)
Gender: Women	*Serve a want* (clothing is brand name only, and has a higher price point than the competition)
Marital Status: Married	
Market Observations: located on Main Street of Anytown, a street that is seeing many new boutiques open up, proximate to the main shopping mall two blocks from popular mid-range restaurant that is busy at lunch	**Industry Predictions:** large number of new housing developments in the city and surrounding areas two new schools in construction expect to see an influx of new families move to town from Anycity
Competition Observations: baby clothing also available at two local department stores, and one second-hand shop on opposite side of town	**Online Research:** half of Anytown's population is female, and 25% have children under the age of 15 years Anytown's population is expected to increase by 32% within three years The average household income for Anytown is $75,000 annually

TARGET MARKET:

The target market can then be described as married mothers with children under five years old, between the ages of 25 and 45, who have recently moved to Anytown from Anycity, and have a household income of at least $100K annually.

Target Market Sample 2: B2B Market

Business: Confidential Paper Shredding	**Target Business Size:** Small to medium
Market Type: B2B (Business to Business)	**Target Business Revenue:** $500K to $1M
Business Purpose: *Meet an operations need* (provide confidential on-site shredding services for business documents)	**Target Business Type:** produce or handle a variety of sensitive paper documentation accountants, lawyers, real estate agents, etc.
Market Observations: there are two main areas of office buildings and industrial warehouses in Anycity three more office towers are being constructed, and will be completed this year	**Industry Predictions:** the professional sector is seeing revenue growth of 24% over last year, which indicates increased client billing and staff recruitment
Competition Observations: one confidential shredding company serves the region, covering Anycity and the surrounding towns provide regular (weekly or biweekly) service, but does not have the capacity to handle large volumes at one time	**Online Research:** Anycity's biggest employment sectors are: manufacturing, tourism, food services, and professional services

TARGET MARKET:

The target market can then be described as small to medium sized businesses in the professional sector with an annual revenue of $500K to $1M who require both regular and infrequent large volume paper shredding services.

Segmenting Your Market

Your market segments are the groups within your target market – broken down by a determinant in one of the following four categories:

- Demographics
- Psychographics
- Geographics
- Behaviors

Segmenting your target market into several more specific groups allows you to further tailor your marketing campaign and more specifically position your product or service. You may wish to divide your ad campaign into four sections, and target four specific markets with messages that will most resonate with the audience.

For example, the baby clothing store may choose to segment its target market by psychographics, or lifestyle. If the larger target market is *married females with children under five, between the ages of 25 and 45, who have a household income of at least $100K annually*, it can be broken down into the following lifestyle segments:

- Fitness-oriented mothers
- Career-oriented mothers
- New mothers

With these three categories, unique marketing messages can be created that speak to the hot-buttons of each segment. The more accurate and specific you can make communications with your target market, the greater impact you will have on your revenues.

Market Segmentation Variables

Demographic	Psychographic	Geographic	Behavioristic
Age	Personality	Region	Brand Loyalty
Income	Lifestyle	Country	Product Usage
Gender	Values	City	Purchase
Generation	Attitude	Area	Frequency
Nationality	Motivation	Neighborhood	Profitability
Ethnicity	Activities	Density	Readiness to Buy
Marital Status	Interests	Climate	User Status
Family Size			
Occupation			
Religion			
Language			
Education			
Employment Type			
Housing Type			
Housing Ownership			
Political Affiliation			

Understanding Your Target Market

Once you have determined who your market is, make a point of learning everything you can about them. You need to have a strong understanding of who they are, what they like, where they shop, why they buy, and how they spend their time. Remind yourself that you may *think* you know your market, but until you have verified the information, you'll be driving your marketing strategy blind.

Also be aware that markets change, just like people. Just because you knew your market when you started your business 10 years ago, doesn't mean you know it now. Regular market research is part of any successful business plan, and a great habit to start.

Types of Market Research

Surveys

The simplest way to gather information from your clients or target market is through a survey. You can craft a questionnaire full of questions about your product, service, market demographics, buyer motivations, and so on. Plus, anonymous surveys will produce the most accurate information since names are not attached to the results or specific comments.

Depending on the purpose—whether it is to gather demographic information, product or service feedback, or other data—there are a number of ways to administer a survey.

1. *Telephone*

Telephone surveys are a more time-consuming option, but have the benefit of live communication with your target market. Generally, it is best to have a third party conduct this type of survey to gather the most honest feedback. This is the method that market researchers use for polling, which is highly reliable.

2. *Online*

Online surveys are the easiest to administer yourself. There a many web-based services that quickly and easily allow to you custom create your survey, and send it to your email marketing list. These services can also analyze, summarize and interpret the results on your behalf. Keep in mind that the results include only those who are motivated to respond, which may slant your results.

3. *Paper-based.*

Paper surveys are seldom used, and can prove to be an inefficient method. Like online surveys, your results are based on the feedback of those who were motivated for one reason or another to respond. However, the time and effort involved in taking the survey, filing it out, and returning it to your place of business may deter people from participating.

Keep in mind that surveys can be complex to administer, and consume more time and resources than you have planned. If you have the budget, consider hiring a professional market research firm to lead or assist with the process. This will also ensure that the methodology is standard practice, and will garner the most accurate results.

Website Analysis

Tracking your website traffic is an excellent way to research your existing and potential customer's interests and behavior. From this information, you can ensure the design, structure and content of your website is catering to the people who use it – and the people you want to use it.

User-friendly website traffic analytics programs can easily show you who is visiting your site, where they are from, and what pages of your site they are viewing. Services like Google Analytics can tell you what page they

17

arrive at, where they click to, how much time they spend on each page, and on which page they leave the site.

This is powerful (and free!) information to have in your market research, and easy to monitor monthly or weekly, depending on the needs of your business.

Customer Purchase Data (Consumer Behavior)

If you do not have the budget to conduct your own professional market research, you can use existing resources on consumer behavior. While this data may not be specific to your region or city, general consumer research is actual data that can be helpful in confirming assumptions you may have made about your target market.

Your customer loyalty program or Point of Sale system may also be of help in tracking customer purchases and identifying trends in purchase behavior. If you can track who is buying, what they're buying and how often they're buying, you'll have an arsenal of powerful insight into your existing client base.

Focus Groups

Focus groups look at the psychographic and behavioristic aspects of your target market. Groups of six to 12 people are gathered and asked general and specific questions about their purchase motivations and behaviors. These questions could relate to your business in particular, or to the general industry.

Focus group sessions can also be time consuming to organize and facilitate, so consider hiring the services of a professional market research firm. You may also receive more honest information if a third party is asking the questions, and receiving the responses from focus group participants.

For cost savings, consider partnering with an associate in the same industry who is not a direct competitor, and who would benefit from the same market data.

2

Creating a Powerful Offer

I'm not going to beat around the bush on this one:

Your offer is the granite foundation of your marketing campaign.

Get it right, and everything else will fall into place. Your headline will grab readers, your copy will sing, your ad layout will hardly matter, and you will have customers running to your door.

Get it wrong, and even the best looking, best-written campaign will sink like the Titanic.

A powerful offer is an irresistible offer. It's an offer that gets your audience frothing at the mouth and clamoring over each other all the way to your door. An offer that makes your readers pick up the phone and open their wallets.

Irresistible offers make your potential customers think, "I'd be crazy not to take him up on that," or "An offer like this doesn't come around very often." They instill a sense of emotion, of desire, and ultimately, urgency.

Make it easy for customers to purchase from you the first time, and spend your time keeping them coming back.

I'll say it again: **get it right, and everything else will fall into place.**

The Crux of Your Marketing Campaign

As you work your way through this program, you will find that nearly every chapter discusses the importance of a powerful offer as related to your marketing strategy or promotional campaign.

There's a reason for this. The powerful offer is more often than not the reason a customer will open their wallets. It is how you generate leads, and then convert them into loyal customers. The more dramatic, unbelievable, and valuable the offer is the more dramatic and unbelievable the response will be.

Many companies spend thousands of dollars on impressive marketing campaigns in glossy magazines and big city newspapers. They send massive direct mail campaigns on a regular basis; yet don't receive an impressive or massive response rate.

These companies do not yet understand that simply providing information on their company and the benefits of their product is not enough to get customers to act. There is no reason to pick up the phone or visit the store, *right now*.

Your powerful, irresistible offer can:
- Increase leads
- Drive traffic to your website or business
- Move old product

- Convert leads into customers
- Build your customer database

What Makes a Powerful Offer?

A powerful offer is one that makes the most people respond, and take action. It gets people running to spend money on your product or service.

Powerful offers nearly always have an element of *urgency* and of *scarcity*. They give your audience a reason to act immediately, instead of put it off until a later date.

Urgency relates to time. The offer is only available until a certain date, during a certain period of the day, or if you act within a few hours of seeing the ad. The customer needs to act now to take advantage of the offer.

Scarcity related to quantity. There are only a certain number of customers who will be able to take advantage of the offer. There may be a limited number of spaces, a limited number of products, or simply a limited number of people the business will provide the offer to. Again, this requires that customer acts immediately to reap the high value for low cost.

Powerful offers also:

Offer great value. Customers perceive the offer as having great value – more than a single product on its own, or the product at its regular price. It is clear that the offer takes the reader's needs and wants into consideration.

Make sense to the reader. They are simple and easy to understand if read quickly. Avoid percentages – use half off or 2 for 1 instead of 50% off. There are no "catches" or requirements; no fine print.

Seem logical. The offer doesn't come out of thin air. There is a logical reason behind it – a holiday, end of season, anniversary celebration, or new product. People can get suspicious of offers that seem "too good to be true" and have no apparent purpose.

Provide a premium. The offer provides something extra to the customer, like a free gift, or free product or service. They feel they are getting something extra for no extra cost. Premiums are perceived to have more value than discounts.

Remember that when your target market reads your offer, they will be asking the following questions:

1. What are you offering me?
2. What's in it for me?
3. What makes me sure I can believe you?
4. How much do I have to pay for it?

The Most Powerful Types of Offers

Decide what kind of offer will most effectively achieve your objectives. Are you trying to generate leads, convert customers, build a database, move old product off the shelves, or increase sales?

Consider what type of offer will be of most value to your ideal customers – what offer will make them act quickly.

Free Offer

This type of offer asks customers to act immediately in exchange for something free. This is a good strategy to use to build a customer database or mailing list. Offer a free consultation, free consumer report, or other item of low cost to you but of high perceived value.

You can also advertise the value of the item you are offering for free. For example, act now and you'll receive a free consultation, worth $75 dollars. This will dramatically increase your lead generation, and allow you to focus on conversion when the customer comes through the door or picks up the phone.

The Value Added Offer

Add additional services or products that cost you very little, and combine them with other items to increase their attractiveness. This increases the perception of value in the customer's mind, which will justify increasing the price of a product or service without incurring extra hard costs to your business.

Package Offer

Package your products or services together in a logical way to increase the perceived value as a whole. Discount the value of the package by a small margin, and position it as a "start-up kit" or "special package." By packaging goods of mixed values, you will be able to close more high-value sales. For example: including a free desk-jet printer with every computer purchase.

Premium Offer

Offer a bonus product or service with the purchase of another. This strategy will serve your bottom line much better than discounting. This includes 2 for 1 offers, offers that include free gifts, and in-store credit with purchases over a specific dollar amount.

Urgency Offer

As I mentioned above, offers that include an element of urgency enjoy a better response rate, as there is a reason for your customers to act immediately. Give the offer a deadline or limit the number of spots available.

Guarantee Offer

Offer to take the risk of making a purchase away from your customers. Guarantee the performance or results of your product or service, and offer to compensate the customer with their money back if they are not satisfied. This will help overcome any fear or reservations about your product, and make it more likely for your leads to become customers.

Create Your Powerful Offer

1. Pick a single product or service.

Focus on only one product or service – or one product or service *type* – at a time. This will keep your offer clear, simple, and easy to understand. This can be an area of your business you wish to grow, or old product that you need to move off the shelves.

2. Decide what you want your customers to do.

What are you looking to achieve from your offer? If it is to generate more leads, then you'll need your customer to contact you. If it is to quickly sell old product, you'll need your customer to come into the store and buy it. Do you want them to visit your website? Sign up for your newsletter? How long do they have to act? Be clear about your call to action, and state it clearly in your offer.

3. Dream up the biggest, best offer.

First, think of the biggest, best things you could offer your customers – regardless of cost and ability. Don't limit yourself to a single type of offer, combine several types of offers to increase value. Offer a premium, plus a guarantee, with a package offer. Then take a look at what you've created, and make the necessary changes so it is realistic.

4. Run the numbers.

Finally, make sure the offer will leave you with some profit – or at least allow you to break even. You don't want to publish an outrageous offer that will generate a tremendous number of leads, but leave you broke. Remember that each customer has an acquisition cost, as well as a lifetime value. The amount of their first purchase may allow you to break even, but the amount of their subsequent purchases may make you a lovely profit.

3

Risk Reversal to Increase Sales

What is the biggest objection you need to overcome when closing a sale? Is it cost? Belief in what you have to say? Confidence in your product or service?

While it is a different answer for every business, every business has to deal with some element of customer fear or hesitation before a monetary transaction.

The reality is that even if you overcome these objections and close the sale, your customer walks away carrying 99% of the risk associated with the purchase. If the product doesn't work, breaks down, or doesn't perform to expectations, your customer has parted with their dollars in exchange for disappointment.

In marketing, your objective is to generate as many leads as possible, then to convert each lead into a customer, or sale. The ratio of leads to closed sales is called your conversion rate.

What if you could eliminate the risk involved in a transaction? Would you turn more leads into customers? The answer is absolutely.

Introducing a risk reversal element into your marketing message or unique offer is a powerful way to give yourself an edge on the competition and close more sales. But how exactly are you going to do this?

It's easy – just give them a guarantee.

The Power of Guarantees

What is Risk Reversal?

Risk reversal simply refers to reversing the risk associated with a transaction – transferring it from the customer to the vendor.

Everyone can think of a handful of times they have purchased a product or service that did not deliver on their expectations. A time where a salesperson made them a promise and did not deliver. A time where they *lost money* on a faulty product or bogus service.

Fear of being burned or taken advantage of prevents many people from spending their money. Customers can also be very wary of buying a product or service for the first time.

Providing a strong guarantee eliminates the majority of risk involved in the purchase, and breaks down natural barriers in the sales process. Guarantees will often shorten the sales process all together – skipping any discussion of objections – because the customer does not see any risk in "trying the product out."

There is also a growing consumer expectation when it comes to guarantees. Many stores will take back anything the customer has not been happy with, and return money or store credit. Popular health food stores encourage customers to try new or unfamiliar products by promising a hassle-free, no questions asked return process. A guarantee or easy return policy can be the difference between choosing one business over its competition.

Your customers buy results, not products or services

The strongest guarantee you can make is on *results*, not products or services.

If you guarantee that your customer will receive the benefits or results they are looking for, the specific product or service they'll need to achieve those results becomes irrelevant.

People buy benefits and results. For example, they don't buy water purifiers; they buy the benefit enjoying clean, fresh-tasting water. They don't buy lawn sprinkler systems; they buy a healthy green lawn.

Once you understand what specific benefit or solution your customers are seeking, find a way to guarantee they'll receive or experience that solution. If they don't, you'll compensate them for it.

Remember what you have guaranteed

While guarantees will increase sales for most businesses, they can also be the fast track to business failure if their product or service isn't a quality one. Take the time to ensure you have a strong offering before you implement a guarantee.

Guarantees are most effective when you are selling someone something they need or want – not when you are trying to convince someone to purchase something they have no use for.

Increasing Conversion Rates with a Guarantee

Guarantees can help your business turn more qualified leads into repeat customers. Strong guarantees are big and bold, but also realistic. They're just a little bit better than your competition, but consistent with the industry's standards.

Your conversion rate

Your conversion rate is the percentage of clients you convert from leads into customers. The higher your conversion rate, the more revenue you will generate.

To figure out your conversion rate, divide the number of people who purchase from you by the number of people who inquired about your product or service. This will generate a percentage value of your conversion rate.

Guarantees encourage and increase conversion. They motivate potential customers to buy – and to buy from you – because you stand behind what you sell in a big way. There is no risk involved in purchasing what you have to offer.

Creating your guarantee

So you're convinced your business – and your customers – would benefit from a strong guarantee. Now what? What are you going to guarantee? How are you going to position it?

Once again, this goes back to your target audience and your product or service. What are some of the major objections your potential customers raise during the sales process? What kind of risk do they take on when they make a purchase? How much time will they need to test or experience your product or service?

Brainstorm a list of things about your industry that really frustrate your customers. They could be service-based (contractors that don't show up, employees who don't perform) or product-based (products that break, do not perform). Then, take a look at your list and decide how you can make sure these things do not happen. Think big – you can do a lot more than you think – then determine if you can actually make good on your promise. If you can't guarantee the first frustration, then move on to the second.

Here are some tips on writing your guarantee:

- **Be specific**. Explain exactly what you are guaranteeing. Don't make vague guarantees that a product will "work" or a service will make you "happy". These words mean different things to different people. Guarantee specific performance or results.

- **Include a clear timeframe.** Put a realistic timeframe on your guarantee. Very few products or services are good forever. Offer a 30-day or 90-day free trial; guarantee results within a set number of days or weeks. This can protect your company, and sets out clear expectations for your clients.

- **Be bold**. Unbelievable guarantees get a customer's attention, so go as far as you realistically can with your claim. Find a way to stand out over the competition – which may also have a guarantee.

- **Tell them what you'll do**. Explain what you'll do – how you'll compensate them – if your product or service doesn't deliver. Be specific, talk money, and go above and beyond.

Implementing guarantees

Tell your clients!

Put your guarantee everywhere – your website, brochures, receipt tape, in-store signage, advertisements, and other promotional materials. It will only help attract customers if they know about it.

Send a newsletter to your existing client base informing them of your new guarantees – you never know how many customers you can convince to come back and spend more in your business.

Train your Staff

Once you have decided to offer your clients a guarantee, you need to ensure your staff are properly trained on the specific policies and procedures associated with that guarantee. If you offer different guarantees for different products and services, ensure this is made clear as well.

Presumably, your staff will be communicating the details of your guarantee, and fielding customer questions. They will have to know how to sell the product using the guarantee as a benefit, and understand every application of the guarantee in your business. Every scenario a customer may need to use it.

To ensure your staff is not making any false claims or promises, create a guarantee script for them to use and stick to. This will prevent customers from returning with false hopes for their money back, or other compensation.

Returns + Claims

So, by now you must be thinking, "Great, I can convert more customers with a strong guarantee, and increase my sales. But what about the added risk I have taken on from my customers? Won't I start to see a ton of returns and service claims?" This is a valid question. Making a strong guarantee means standing by it and delivering on your promise. Inevitably, when you guarantee something, someone is going to take you up on that guarantee and make a claim. I'm going to answer this question in two parts:

1. Stand behind your product or service. You're not in business to scam customers. If you sell a product or service, and you believe in it enough to offer it to your customers, it is likely a quality product or genuine service.

If this is a concern to you, consider implementing strong quality controls or stronger criteria for your merchandising. Companies that offer products and services that deliver results can offer the strongest guarantees.

Of course you will get returns. You will have customers come in to take advantage of you. Just remember that as long as the increase in sales outweighs the claims, your guarantee strategy has been successful.

2. Understand your customer's likely behavior. The truth is that most customers will never take advantage of your guarantee – regardless of their satisfaction level. There are a number of reasons for this.

The first is that most people can't be bothered to drive, mail, or otherwise seek a refund on an item under $50. Many let the timeframe slip by, and have an "oh well" attitude.

The second is that most people don't like confrontation. There is usually an element of confrontation involved in telling someone you didn't like a product or service, and many people do not have the confidence to do so. They'd rather eat the cost than go through the process of asking for a refund.

Handling claims and returns:

If you do have your product returned, it is in your company's best interest to create a system for handling these customer interactions.

Create a claim form

Ensure that each customer who makes a claim about your product or service fills out a standard form. Doing so will help you prevent fraud, gather important information about the customer and their reasoning, and create a "hoop" for the customer to jump through if they want their money back.

Name

Date

Contact Information

Salesperson

Product

Reason for claim:

Comments

Follow-up

Keep a claim or return log

Create a log or filing system for your claims. This will give you a snapshot of your guarantee program, a record-keeping system, and a wealth of information about each customer's experience and motivations.

Use the information

Take the claim forms your customers have filled out, and review them regularly. While some of the claims won't be genuine, there will be some real feedback you can use to improve your product or service, or to modify your guarantee. You may need to make it more realistic, or change the specifics.

4

Generating an Unlimited Amount of Leads for Your Business

Where do your customers come from?

Most people would probably choose advertising as an answer. Or referrals. Or direct mail campaigns. This may seem true, but it's not really accurate.

Your customers come from leads that have been turned into sales. Each customer goes through a two-step process before they arrive with their wallets open. They have been converted from a member of a target market, to a lead, then to a customer.

So, would it not stand to reason then, that when you advertise or send any marketing material out to your target market, that you're not really trying to generate customers? That instead, you're trying to generate leads?

When you look at your marketing campaign from this perspective, the idea of generating leads as compared to customers seems a lot less daunting. The pressure of closing sales is no longer placed on advertisements or brochures.

From this perspective, the **general purpose of your advertising and marketing efforts is then to generate leads from qualified customers.** Seems easy enough, doesn't it?

Where Are Your Leads Coming From?

If I asked you to tell me the top three ways you generate new sales leads, what would you say?

- Advertising?
- Word of mouth?
- Networking?
- …don't know?

The first step toward increasing your leads is in understanding how many leads you currently get on a regular basis, as well as where they come from. Otherwise, how will you know when you're getting more phone calls or walk-in customers?

If you don't know where your leads come from, start *today.* Start asking every customer that comes through your door, "how did you hear about us?" or "what brought you in today?" Ask every customer that calls where they found your telephone number, or email address. Then, *record the information for at least an entire week.*

When you're finished, take a look at your spreadsheet and write your top three lead generators here:

1. _____

2. _____

3. _____

From Lead to Customer: Conversion Rates

Leads mean nothing to your business unless you convert them into customers. You could get hundreds of leads from a single advertisement, but unless those leads result in purchases, it's been a largely unsuccessful (and costly) campaign.

The ratio of leads (potential customers) to transactions (actual customers) is called your conversion rate. Simply divide the number of customers who actually purchased something by the number of customers who inquired about your product or service, and multiply by 100.

 # transactions / # leads x 100 = % conversion rate

If, in a given week, I have 879 customers come into my store, and 143 of them purchase something, the formula would look like this:

[143 (customers) / 879 (leads)] x 100 = 16.25% conversion rate

What's Your Conversion Rate?

Based on the formula above, you can see that the higher your conversion rate, the more profitable the business.

Your next step is to determine you own current conversion rate. Add up the number of leads you sourced in the last section, and divide that number into the total transactions that took place in the same week.

Write your conversion rate here:

_____.

Quality (or Qualified) Leads

Based on our review of conversion rates, we can see that the number of leads you generate means nothing unless those leads are being converted into customers.

So what affects your ability (and the ability of your team) to turn leads into customers? Do you need to improve your scripts? Your product or service? Find a more competitive edge in the marketplace?

Maybe. But the first step toward increasing conversion rates is to evaluate the leads you are currently generating, and make sure those leads are the right ones.

What are Quality Leads?

Potential customers are potential customers, right? Anyone who walks into your store or picks up the phone to call your business could be convinced to purchase from you, right? Not necessarily, but this is a common assumption most business owners make.

Quality leads are the people who are the most likely to buy your product or service. They are the qualified buyers who comprise your target market. Anyone might walk in off the street to browse a furniture store – regardless of whether or not they are in the market for a new couch or bed frame. This lead is solely interested in browsing, and is not likely to be converted to a customer.

A quality lead would be someone looking for a new kitchen table, and who specifically drove to that same furniture because a friend had raved about the service they received that month. **These are the kinds of leads you need to focus on generating.**

How Do You Get Quality Leads?

- **Know your target market**. Get a handle on who your customers are – the people who are most likely to buy your product or service. Know their age, sex, income, and purchase motivations. From that information you can determine how best to reach your specific audience.

- **Focus on the 80/20 rule.** A common statistic in business is that 80% of your revenue comes from 20% of your customers. These are your star clients, or your ideal clients. These are the clients you should focus your efforts on recruiting. This is the easiest way to grow your business and your income.

- **Get specific.** Focus not only on who you want to attract, but how you're going to attract them. If you're trying to generate leads from a specific market segment, craft a unique offer to get their attention.

- **Be proactive**. Once you've generated a slew of leads, make sure you have the resources to follow up on them. Be diligent and aggressive, and follow up in a timely manner. You've done to work to get them, now reel them in.

Get More Leads from Your Existing Strategies

Increasing your lead generation doesn't necessarily mean diving in and implementing an expensive array of new marketing strategies. Marketing and customer outreach for the purpose of lead generation can be inexpensive, and bring a high return on investment.

You are likely already implementing many of these strategies. With a little tweaking or refinement, you can easily double your leads, and ensure they are more qualified.

Here are some popular ways to generate quality leads:

Direct Mail to Your Ideal Customers

Direct mail is one of the fastest and most effective ways to generate leads that will build your business. It's a simple strategy – in fact, you're probably already reaching out to potential clients through direct mail letters with enticing offers.

The secret to doubling your results is to craft your direct mail campaigns specifically for a highly targeted audience of your *ideal* customers.

Your ideal customers are the people who will buy the most of your products or services. They are the customers who will buy from you over and over again, and refer your business to their friends. They are the group of 20% of your clients who make up 80% of your revenue.

Identify your ideal customers

Who are your ideal customers? What is their age, sex, income, location and purchase motivation? Where do they live? How do they spend their money? Be as specific as possible.

Once you have identified who your ideal customers are, you can begin to determine how you can go about reaching them. Will you mail to households or apartment buildings? Families or retirees? Direct mail lists are available for purchase from a wide range of companies, and can be segregated into a variety of demographic and sociographic categories.

Craft a special offer

Create an offer that's too good to refuse – not for your entire target market, but for your ideal customer. How can you cater to their unique needs and wants? What will be irresistible for them?

For example, if you operate a furniture store, your target market is a broad range of people. However, if you are targeting young families, your offer will be much different than one you may craft for empty-nesters.

Court them for their business

Don't stop at a single mail-out. Sometimes people will throw your letter away two or three times before they are motivated to act. Treat your direct mail campaign like a courtship, and understand that it will happen over time.

First send a letter introducing yourself, and your irresistible offer. Then follow up on a monthly basis with additional letters, newsletters, offers, or flyers. Repetition and reinforcement of your presence is how your customer will go from saying, "who is this company" to "I buy from this company."

Advertise for lead generation

Statistics show that nearly 50% of all purchase decisions are motivated by advertising. It can also be a relatively cost effective way of generating leads.

We've already discussed the importance of ensuring your advertisements are purpose-focused. The general purpose of most advertisements is to increase sales – which starts with leads. However ads that are created solely for lead generation – that is, to get the customers to pick up the phone or walk in the store – are a category of their own.

Lead generation ads are simply designed and create a sense of curiosity or mystery. Often, they feature an almost unbelievable offer. Their purpose is not to convince the customer to buy, but to contact the business for more information.

As always, when you are targeting your ideal audience, you'll need to ensure that your ads are placed prominently in publications that audience reads. This doesn't mean you have to fork over the cash for expensive display ads. Inexpensive advertising in e-mail newsletters, classifieds, and the yellow pages are very effective for lead generation.

Here are some tips for lead generation advertising:

Leverage low-cost advertising

Place ads in the yellow pages, classifieds section, e-mail newsletters, and online. If your target audience is technology savvy, consider new forms of advertising like Facebook and Google Adwords.

Spark curiosity

Don't give them all the information they need to make a decision. Ask them to contact you for the full story, or the complete details of the seemingly outrageous offer.

Grab them with a killer headline

Like all advertising, a compelling headline is essential. Focus on the greatest benefits to the customer, or feature an unbelievable offer.

Referrals and host beneficiary relationships

A referral system is one of the most profitable systems you can create in your business. The beauty is once it's set up, it often runs itself.

Customers that come to you through referrals are often your "ideal customers." They are already trusting and willing to buy. This is one of the most cost-effective methods of generating new business, and is often the most profitable. These referral clients will buy more, faster, and refer further business to your company.

Referrals naturally happen without much effort for reputable businesses, but with a proactive referral strategy you'll certainly double or triple your referrals. Sometimes, you just need to ask!

Here are some easy strategies you can begin to implement today:

Referral incentives

Give your customers a reason to refer business to you. Reward them with discounts, gifts, or free service in exchange for a successful referral.

Referral program

Offer new customers a free product or service to get them in the door. Then, at the end of the transaction, give them three more 'coupons' for the same free product or service that they can give to their friends. Do the same with their friends. This ongoing program will bring you more business than you can imagine.

Host-beneficiary relationships

Forge alliances with non-competitive companies who target your ideal customers. Create cross-promotion and cross-referral direct mail campaigns that benefit both businesses.

Lead Management Systems

Once your lead generation strategies are in place, you'll also need a system to manage incoming inquiries. You'll need to ensure you receive enough information from each lead to follow up on at a later date. You'll also need to create a system to organize that information, and track the lead as it is converted into a sale.

Gathering Information from Your Leads

Here is a list of information you should gather from your leads. This list can be customized to the needs of your business, and the type of information you can realistically ask for from your potential customers.

- Company Name
- Name of Contact
- Alternate Contact Person
- Mailing Address
- Phone Number
- Fax Number

- Cell Phone
- Email Address
- Website Address
- Product of Interest
- Other Competitors Engage

Lead List Management Methods:

Once you have gathered information from your lead, you'll need a system to organize their information and keep a detailed contact history.

The simplest way to do this is with a database program, but you can also use a variety of hard copy methods.

Electronic Database Programs

- High level of organization available
- Unlimited space for notes and record-keeping
- Data-entry required
- Examples include: MS Outlook, MS Excel, Maximizer
- Customer Relationship Management Software

Index Cards

- Variety of sizes: 3x5, 4X6 or 5X8
- Basic contact information on one side
- Notes on the other side
- Easy to organize and sort

Rolodex System

- Maintain more contacts than index card system
- Easily organized and compact
- Basic contact information on one side
- Notes on the other side
- Can keep phone conversation and purchase details

Notebook

- Best if leads are managed by a single person
- Lots of room for notes
- Inexpensive
- Difficult to re-organize
- Best for smaller lists

Business Card Organizer

- Best for small lists – under 100
- Limited space for notes
- No data entry required
- Rolodex-style, or clear binder pages

5

How to Create Repeat Business and Have Clients that Pay, Stay and Refer

When it comes to marketing and generating more income, most business owners are focused outward.

They've carefully established and segmented their target market, and created specific offers and messages for each market segment. They spend thousands of dollars in advertising and direct mail campaigns in hot pursuit of more leads, more customers, and more foot traffic.

While this is an effective way to build a business, it is costly and time consuming. It requires constant and consistent effort, and while this approach does generate results, those results quickly disappear when the effort stops or becomes less intense.

Successful businesses that see sustained growth have a double-edged marketing strategy. They focus their efforts *outward* – on new potential customers and marketing – as well as *inward* – on existing customers and referral business.

These successful businesses have leveraged their existing efforts to generate more revenue. Simply put, their customers buy from them over and over again.

For most businesses, this is the easiest way to increase their revenues. Simple customer loyalty strategies and outstanding customer service are often all you need to dramatically increase your sales – from the customers you already have.

The Cost of Your Customers

Do you know how much it costs your business to buy new customers?

Each new customer that walks through your door – with the exception of referrals – has cost you money to acquire. You have spent money on advertising and promotions to generate leads and turn those leads into customers.

For example, if you have placed an ad in your local newspaper for $1,000, and the ad brings in 10 customers, you have paid $100 to acquire each customer. You would need to ensure each of those customers spent at least $200 to cover your margin and break even.

Alternately, if you spent two hours of your time and $10 per month on an email marketing program to send a newsletter to your existing database of customers, and you bring in 10 customers as a result – each customer has cost you $1.

Generating more repeat business means focusing on the marketing strategies that aim to keep your existing customers instead of purchase new ones – effectively reducing the cost of attracting new customers to your business.

These strategies are simple to implement, and don't require much time investment. Just a solid understanding of how to make customers want to come back and spend more of their money

Keeping Your Customers

Marketing strategies that focus on keeping your current customer base are easy and enjoyable to implement. They allow you to build real relationships with the people you do business with, instead of dealing with a revolving door of people on the other end of your sales process.

Repeat customers create a community of people around your business that presumably share the same needs, desires and frustrations. The information you gain from these customers (market research) can help you strengthen your understanding of your target audience, and more accurately segment it.

Remember – 80% of your revenue comes from 20% of your customers. Always focus on these customers. They are ideal customers that you want to recruit, and hold on to.

Customer Service: Make them love buying from you

Every business – even those with excellent service standards can improve the service they provide their customers. Customer service seems to be a dying concept in most businesses; more focus seems to be placed on the speed of the transaction. These days you can even go to the grocery store now and not speak to a single sales associate thanks to self-serve checkouts.

To improve your company's customer service standards, take a survey of your customers and your employees to brainstorm ways you can improve the experience of buying from your business.

Successful customer service standards – those that make your customers *buy* – are:

Consistent. The standards are up kept by every person in your organization. Expectations are clear and followed through. Customers know what to expect, and choose your business because of those expectations.

Convenient. It is nearly effortless for the customer to spend money at your place of business. Convenience can take many forms – location, product selection, value-added services like delivery – and it is also consistent.

Customer-driven. The service the customer receives is exactly how they would like to be treated when buying your product or service. It is reflective of your target market, and appropriate to their lifestyle. Customers would probably not appreciate white linen tablecloths at a fast food restaurant, but they would appreciate a 2-minutes or less guarantee.

Newsletters: Keep in touch with your customers

A regular newsletter is an easy, time-effective, and inexpensive marketing strategy to implement. Unfortunately, many small businesses think these are too time consuming and too expensive to adopt as part of their marketing strategy.

The most popular type of newsletter distribution is email. This will cost your business as little at $10 per month for an email marketing service subscription, and can be customized to your unique branding.

Here is an easy five-step process to starting a company newsletter:

1. Pick your audience. New customers? Market segment? Existing customers?

2. Choose what you're going to say. Company news? Feature product? New offer?

3. Determine how you're going to say it. Articles? Bullet points? Pictures?

4. Decide how it's going to get to your audience. Email? Mail? In-store?

5. Track your results. How many people opened it? Read it? Took action?

Value Added Service: Give them happy surprises

Adding value to your business is an effective way of getting your customers back. Every person I know would choose a mattress store that offered free delivery over one that did not. It's that simple.

There are many ways to add value to your business, including:

o **Feature your expertise.** Use your knowledge to provide additional value to your customers. Offer a free consumer guide or report with every purchase.

o **Add convenience services.** Offer a service that makes their purchase easier, or more convenient. The best example of this is free shipping or delivery.

o **Package complementary services**. Packaging like items together creates an increase in perceived value. This is great for start-up kits.

o **Offer new products or services**. Feature top of the line or exclusive products, available only at your business. Offer a new service or profile a new staff member with niche expertise.

Value added services generate repeat customers in one of two ways:

1. Impress them on their first visit. Impress you customer with great service, a product that meets their needs, and then wow them with something extra that they weren't expecting. Get them to associate the experience of dealing with your business with happy surprises, and create a perception of higher value.

2. Entice them to come back. The introduction of a new value-added service can be enough to convince a customer to buy from you again. Their initial purchase established a trust and knowledge of your business and its processes. They will want to "be included" in anything new you have to offer – especially if there is exclusivity. It is easier to attract clients that have purchased from you than potential clients who have not.

Customer Loyalty Programs: Give them incentives

Another simple way to keep in touch with existing customers and keep them coming back to you is to create a customer loyalty program.

These programs do not have to be complicated or costly, and are relatively easy to maintain once they have been implemented. These programs help you gain more information on your customers and their purchasing habits.

Here are some examples of simple loyalty programs that you can implement:

Free product or service. Give them every 10th (or 6th) product or service free. Produce stamp cards with your logo and contact information on it.

Reward dollars. Give them a certain percentage of their purchase back in money that can only be spent in-store. Produce "funny money" with your logo and brand.

Rewards points. Give them a certain number of points for every dollar they spend. These points can be spent in-store, or on special items you bring in for points only.

Membership amenities. Give members access to VIP amenities that are not available to other customers. Produce member cards or give out member numbers.

Remember that in order for this strategy to work, you and your team have to understand and promote it. The program in itself becomes a product that you sell.

6

How to Use Testimonials and Profit from Social Proof

The Power of Testimonials

Testimonials are simply the single most powerful asset you can have in your marketing toolkit. When your customers tell others about the benefits of choosing your business, it is a thousand times more powerful than the same words from your mouth.

The words and opinions of others motivate people to spend money every day. From celebrity endorsements on TV and in magazines, to casual conversations with friends, decisions about what product or service to buy – and what brand or provider – are heavily influenced by those who have purchased before.

Why? There are several reasons. Many people have an inherent distrust of salespeople, and a skepticism toward marketing materials. Others are bombarded with choice, and are looking for some sense of security in their purchase decision.

Testimonials build the credibility of your business, break down natural barriers, and create a sense of trust for the consumer. They have an incredible ability to persuade customers to buy, and to buy from you. Think about the last time someone recommended a brand of laundry detergent, a bottle of wine, or a plumber to you. Their positive experience had more of an impact on your decision to buy than any advertisement or discount.

When it comes to spending money, people want a sure bet. They want to know that someone else has bought before, and they want to know that the product or service has delivered the promised results. A testimonial for your business is worth more than any copywriter, clever ad slogan, or sales pitch.

Customers Who Give Testimonials

When people put their name and reputation on paper to endorse something, it creates a sense of loyalty; if questioned, they will back their decision, even if they find later their decision was wrong.

When someone is willing to endorse your product or service in writing, they have likely already started a word-of-mouth chain of verbal testimonials about their positive experience. Remember the last time you discovered a chiropractic miracle worker? Or the fastest and cheapest drycleaner? Didn't you tell every one of your friends who could use the service?

By asking a customer for a testimonial, you are asking for their assistance in the growth of your business. When they feel they are truly helping and participating in the development of your company, their sense of pride will mean continuous loyalty to your product or service.

11 Ways to Get Great Testimonials

Testimonials are powerful – no question. But how do you make sure that the quotes you get from your customers will bring you the most value? How do you ensure that your client will articulate your product's merits in a clear and easy to understand way? How do you make sure you can actually use their testimonials in your marketing materials?

Asking for testimonials requires more effort than merely soliciting general comments and praise. You want to ensure that your customer feels a sense of pride and loyalty in providing their opinion, and that their opinion will have an impact on potential buyers.

How? Glad you asked. Here are 11 proven ways to get great testimonials from your customers.

1. Don't wait!

Your customers are the happiest and most willing to help you within a day to a week of their purchase, so aim to secure the testimonial in this time period. Ask for the testimonial before they leave, and make sure you have all their contact details to follow up with. This also ensures you stay on top of your testimonial recruitment!

2. Get specific

Specific testimonials are more believable. The more specific you can have your customer be, the stronger and more impactful the testimonial will be. Remember the Sleep Country testimonials that referenced the little "booties" that their delivery men wore to keep carpets clean? Meaningful details get remembered. Ask for mention of things like time, dates, extraordinary customer service, and personal observations.

3. If you were the solution – what was the problem?

Testimonials that tell stories are more engaging. Ask client to not only describe their experience with your company, but also the negative experience that led them to your door. If they can describe the struggles and challenges they were facing before receiving your service, the reader will likely be able to sympathize and resonate with similar struggles. This will motivate them to solve their problems with your solution.

4. Write the first draft

Make it easy for your clients. This technique is something you can offer someone who is hesitant to commit to writing a testimonial due to time constraints, or is procrastinating. Ask them to brainstorm a few notes they would like to include in their feedback, write them down, and string them into a concise testimonial for their review. All they have to do is review, print on their letterhead, sign, and mail back to you!

5. Include your marketing message or USP

Always ask your customers to include your unique selling proposition (USP) in the testimonial. For instance, if your USP includes exceptional customer service, same-day installation, and a money-back guarantee then ask your customer to attest to those qualities.

6. A picture says...

Yes, you know the saying. But it's true. When readers attach an image of the speaker to words, the words are enlivened and have twice as much validity and impact. When readers see an image of a previous client using your product or service, their words and opinions are even more believable. You can take these simple pictures yourself – and take many so you have a selection to choose from.

7. Credentials equal trust

As we mentioned, testimonials from credible sources will have the most believability and impact. When you ask for a testimonial, make sure your customer states their expertise and credentials. If you sell custom orthotics, and can secure a solid testimonial from a doctor, their words will be golden in your marketing materials.

8. Don't forget to ask permission

When you ask for testimonials, make sure you are clear that their words may be used in your marketing materials, including advertisements, website and in-store displays. This is a good time to thank them for their time and sincerity, and show your appreciation for their words.

9. Location, location…

Depending on the market reach of your business, the location of your customers is an important part of the believability of your testimonial. If you own a community-based business, when potential clients see you've made others happy just down their street they'll be motivated to use your service too. If you own a regional business, then the cities and addresses of other happy customers can help communicate the reach of your service.

10. Testimonials are not surveys

Keep the purpose of your request in mind when you're asking for testimonials. Testimonials should be positive fodder for your advertising materials. Surveys are used to solicit meaningful (and often confidential) customer information to refine and improve your service. Testimonials are public statements, while surveys are often anonymous and can produce less-than-positive results.

11. Say thank you!

Thanking a customer for their time and effort creating your testimonial is just plain good manners. It also increases loyalty and goodwill. This can be done via email, but sending a formal letter on your letterhead is a more meaningful approach.

Using Testimonials Strategically

So now you have a pile of glowing customer testimonials. What's next?

Choose the most powerful piece of the testimonial

What is the most convincing aspect of the testimonial? Is it the author? Where they are from? A specific sentence or paragraph they wrote? Be strategic about the aspect of the testimonial that you feature, and select what will have the most impact.

For example, you can compile a list titled *What Customers are Saying*, and list only the phrases that support your specific marketing message. Or you can feature the unique credentials or story of your customer, before you even include their testimonial. You can also summarize the testimonial with a powerful headline.

Put them on your website

Adding a page of testimonials to your website is a great start, especially when you're beginning to solicit customer responses. However, the most powerful way to ensure site visitors actually see your testimonials is to include them on every page – especially the ones with the highest traffic.

A testimonial should be placed wherever you make a strong statement about your service or product, and wherever the service or product is described. This is a great way to break up your sales copy with some "proof". As they read about your offering, your credibility will be validated by someone other than you.

Compile your best 25 to 50 letters in a display book

Like a proud grandparent, keep a book of testimonials in the waiting area of your office, your boardroom, and in your desk. Or, put one at the service counter, cash register and anywhere else people may have a moment to flip through.

I've seen this done in recruiting firm, a hardware store, and a physiotherapist's office. When clients have a chance to read the positive experiences of others, they will be more open to hearing your sales pitch less guarded when responding to your unique offering.

Hang your favorite testimonials in your store or office

Testimonials as art! Frame your favorite testimonials – preferably the ones written on client letterhead – and post them on the wall in your business. Even if clients don't read them up close, the volume and visual recognition of client logos will have impact. Plus – your next satisfied clients will want to see their company names on the wall too.

Put them in your advertisements

Use short, clear, concise testimonials in your advertising. When was the last time you saw a prescription drug advertisement without a testimonial? Can't remember? That's because you haven't. The best advertisers know that testimonials are the fastest and most effective way to overcome skepticism and get clients thinking that your product or service is the solution to their problem.

Include a page of testimonials in your direct mail

When sending your marketing materials directly to a mass list of potential clients, let the words of others speak to the merits of your product or service. Put together a page or two of testimonials, and attach it to your mailing. The credibility of your company will be instantly established, encouraging clients to act – and buy – faster.

Partner with an associate for joint mailing

If you have an associate or colleague who has a similar customer base of new prospects for your business, try a joint-endorsed mailing. Each of you will send a letter to your own clients, endorsing the other's products and services. Your service or solution is offered to a potential client by a trusted source, and you are offering your existing clients the added value of an associate's service to complement your own.

Testimonial Request Letter

Here is an example of a basic testimonial request letter that can be customized and made into a template for your unique business. This can also be sent over email if that is how your clients prefer to be contacted.

Mr. John Smith
1234 Main Street

Anytown, Anyplace 90210

January 2, 2006

Dear Mr. Smith,

Thank you for visiting our store this week. It was a pleasure helping you select a new laptop for your daughter to use at university this fall – they just grow up too fast! Your research and clear idea of the product you were searching for truly made our job easy. We love the back to school season, because it means working with clients like yourself.

We know there are a lot of choices when it comes to purchasing a laptop in Anytown, so thank you for choosing ABC Company. If there is anything else we can assist you with, please don't hesitate to contact me directly.

We occasionally ask select customers for their feedback in the form of a testimonial. Because we are so proud of the feedback we receive, we often use our customer's quotes in our marketing materials – specifically our website and sales brochures. The real life experiences of our customers at ABC Company are stories that we are proud of.

Could I ask you to write down some of your feedback? A few words about your experience with ABC Company, and how we helped you and your daughter would be greatly appreciated. We encourage you to print this on your company letterhead, so we can provide your own company with some exposure as well.

You may want to include the names of the associates who helped you, and how your daughter is enjoying her laptop. Again, we would like to feature your name and experience in our marketing materials. For your convenience, I've included a prepaid envelope with which to mail your testimonial back to us.

Thank you very much for your assistance.

Kind regards,

Your name here

Testimonial Thank You Letter

Here is an example of a short thank you letter for a testimonial that can also be customized and made into a template for your unique business. You may wish to write your thank you letters on company note cards, but try to avoid sending these thank you's via email.

Mr. John Smith
1234 Main Street
Anytown, Anyplace 90210

January 10, 2006

Dear Mr. Smith,

We received your glowing testimonial in the mail today, and I wanted to thank you personally for your kind words. Your comments about our store and our people are important to us, and I will make sure my staff takes a moment to read your letter.

We are thrilled that your daughter is enjoying her laptop, and using it to keep in touch with you while she studies abroad. When we sold it to you, we truly believed it would provide the most long-lasting value for her student budget. I hope it serves her for the rest of her time at school.

Thank you again for taking the time to write us. We are all proud to have been of service to you and your daughter, and look forward to seeing you both again soon.

Warm regards,

Your Name Here

Testimonial Examples

Below you will find a series of sample testimonials, and excerpts from testimonial letters. Read these over, and take a moment to notice why each is a powerful statement. We have also summarized each testimonial with a headline.

24% Response Rate from a Single Direct Mailing!

We were skeptical about direct mail campaigns, and unsure about the return on investment. Your strategic advice and logistical help made the project run smoothly and easily – we received over 200 leads from this single effort!

John and Betty McFee
Scottsdale, AZ

Best Sleep in 20 Years!

I can't tell you how much I appreciated Craig's patience and assistance in my mattress selection. He is so knowledgeable of each mattress' design and features, and helped us find a financing solution that worked with our budget. I haven't slept this well in over two decades. Promote him!

Jason Carmichael

Gentle and effective approach

I have always been reluctant to visit a chiropractor for my lower back pain because I am not comfortable with physical adjustments. Sarah took the time to clearly explain the cause of my pain, and gave me easy exercises to help correct the problem. She respected my comfort level, and treated me without uncomfortable cracks and snaps!

Wally Orton

Testimonial Worksheet

Start today! Brainstorm a list of recent customers and clients who you will approach for testimonials. Post this worksheet in your office, and track your progress. Aim for 50 testimonials in two months. You can never have too many.

Name + Phone	Request Letter Sent	Follow Up Call Made	Testimonial Received	Thank-you Letter Sent
	☐	☐	☐	☐
	☐	☐	☐	☐
	☐	☐	☐	☐
	☐	☐	☐	☐
	☐	☐	☐	☐
	☐	☐	☐	☐
	☐	☐	☐	☐
	☐	☐	☐	☐
	☐	☐	☐	☐
	☐	☐	☐	☐
	☐	☐	☐	☐
	☐	☐	☐	☐
	☐	☐	☐	☐
	☐	☐	☐	☐
	☐	☐	☐	☐
	☐	☐	☐	☐
	☐	☐	☐	☐
	☐	☐	☐	☐

7

How to Double your Referrals

What if I told you that you could put an inexpensive system in place that would effectively allow your business to growth itself?

For most business owners, a large part of their customer base is comprised of referral customers. These people found out about the company's products or services from the recommendation of a friend or colleague who had a positive experience purchasing from that company.

If your business benefits from referral customers, you will find that these customers arrive ready to buy from you, and tend to buy more often. They also tend to be highly loyal to your product or service.

Seem like great customers to have, don't they?

Referral customers cost less to acquire. Compared to the leads you generate from advertising, direct mail campaigns, and other marketing initiatives, referral customers come to you already qualified and already trusting in the quality of your offering and the respectability of your staff.

With a little effort, and the creation of a formalized system – or strategy – you can not only continue to enjoy referral business, but easily double the number of referral customers that walk through your door. All of this is possible for a minimal investment of time and resources.

Is Your Business a Referral Business?

Referral based businesses benefit from a stream of qualified customers who arrive at their doorstep ready to spend. These businesses put less focus on advertising to generate new leads, and more focus on serving and communicating with their existing customers.

Generally speaking, a referral program can generate outstanding results for nearly any business. Since most referrals do not require any effort, the addition of a strategy and a program will often double or triple the number of qualified referrals that come through a business door.

There are, however, a few types of businesses that will not benefit from a formalized referral strategy. These are businesses with low price points – like fast food restaurants and drugstores. Their customer base is large already, and their efforts would be best spent on increasing the average sale.

A referral program can:

- **Save you time**. Referral strategies – once established – don't require much management or time investment.

- **Deliver more qualified customers**. Your customer arrives with an assumption of trust, and willing to purchase.

- **Improve your reputation.** Your customer's networks likely overlap, and create potential for a single customer to be referred by two people. This encourages the perception that your business is "the place to go."

- **Speed the sales process.** You will have existing common ground and a reputation with the referred customer.

- **Increase your profit.** You will spend less time and money generating leads, and more time serving customers who have their wallets open.

The Cost of Your Customers

As we discussed in the "Repeat Business" section, you don't "get" customers, you *buy* them. The money you spend on advertising, direct mail, and other promotions ideally results in potential customers walking through your doors.

For example, if you placed an ad for $200, and 20 people make a purchase in response to that ad, you would have paid $10 for each customer.

Referral customers cost you next to nothing. Your existing customer does the work of selling your business to their friend or associate, and you benefit from the sale. Aside from the cost of any referral incentives or coupon production, there is no cost involved at all.

Referral customers cost less and require less time investment than any other customer. That means you can spend that time making them a loyal customer, or a devoted fan.

Groom Your Customers

Referral strategies can allow you to groom your customer base. As we have previously discussed, 80% of your revenue comes from 20% of your customers – these are your ideal customers.

These are also the people you have established as your target market, and are the people you cater your marketing and advertising efforts toward.

You also have a group of customers who make up 80% of your headaches. These are the people who complain the most and spend the least.

Use your referral strategy to get more of your *ideal* customers. Spend more time servicing your ideal customers – do everything you can to make them happy – and less time on your headache customers. You can even ask your headache customers to shop elsewhere.

Then, focus your referral efforts on your ideal customers. Ask them to refer business to you, and reward them for doing so. Try to avoid referrals from your headache customers – chances are you'll just get another headache.

Referral Sources

Take some time to brainstorm all the people who could potentially refer business to you. Think beyond your business, to your extracurricular activities and personal life. There are endless sources of people who are ready and willing to send potential customers your way.

Here are some ideas to get you started:

Past Relationships

No, not romantic relationships. I'm talking about anyone you have previously had a relationship with, but for one reason or another have fallen out of touch. This includes former colleagues, associates, customers and friends.

Including them in your referral strategy can be as simple as reaching out through the phone or email, and updating them on your latest business initiative or career move. Gently ask at the end of the correspondence to refer anyone who may need your product or service. They will appreciate that you have attempted to re-establish the relationship.

Suppliers and Vendors

Your suppliers and vendors can be a great source for referrals, because they presumably deal daily with businesses that are complementary to your own. The opportunities to connect two of their customers in a mutually beneficial relationship are endless. These businesses should be happy to help out - especially if you have been a regular and loyal customer.

Customers

Customers are an obvious source of referrals because they are the people who are dealing with you directly on a regular basis. Often, all you have to do is ask and they will happily provide you with contact information of other interested buyers, or contact those buyers themselves.

Your customers also have a high level of product knowledge when it comes to your business, and are in a great position to really sell the strength of your company. Remember from the Testimonials section, the words of your customers are at least 10 times more powerful than any clever headline or marketing piece you could create.

Employees and Associates

Give your employees and associates a reason to have their friends and families shop at your business with a simple incentive program. These people have the most product knowledge, and are in the best position to sell you to a potential customer.

This is also a way to tap into an endless network of people. Who do your employees and associates know? Who do their friends and friends of friends know? A referral chain that connects to your employees can be a highly powerful one.

Competitors

This doesn't seem so obvious, but it can work. Your direct competitors are clearly not the ideal source for referrals. However, indirect competitors can refer their clients or potential clients to you if they cannot meet those clients' needs themselves.

For example, if you sell high end lighting fixtures, the low-budget lighting store down the street may be able to refer clients to you, and vice versa. You may wish to offer a finder's fee or incentive to establish this arrangement.

Your Network

Don't be shy about asking your friends and family members for referrals. Too many people do not provide enough information to their inner circle about what they do or what their business does. This doesn't make sense, since these are the people who should be the most interested!

Take time to explain clearly what your business is all about, and what your point of difference is. Then just ask them if they know anyone who may benefit from what you are offering. You could even provide your friends and family with an incentive – a gift, a meal, or a portion of the sale.

Associations + Special Interest Groups

This is another place you likely have a network of people who have limited knowledge about what you do or what your business does. The advantage here is that you have a group of people with similar belief s and values in the same room. Use it!

The Media

Unless a member of the media is a regular customer of yours, or you are in business to serve the media, this may not seem like an obvious choice either.

The opportunity here is to establish a relationship with an editor or journalist, and position yourself as an expert in your field or industry. Then, next time they are writing a related story, they can ask to quote you and your opinion. When their audience reads the story, they will perceive your business as the industry leader.

Referral Strategies

A referral strategy is any system you can put in place to generate new leads through existing customers. The ideal way to do this is to create a system that runs itself! Here are some ideas for simple strategies you can begin to implement into your business immediately.

Just Ask

This may seem simple and obvious, but it's true. Be open with your customers and associates, and simply ask them if they can refer any of their friends or associates to you. Make it part of doing business with you, and your customers will grow to expect the question. Or, let them know in advance that you'll be asking at a later date.

Remember that this can include potential customers – even if they don't buy from you. The reason they chose not to purchase may have nothing to do with your business; any person who has begun to or actually done business with you can refer to you another person.

Offer Incentives

When you speak to your customers, when you ask them for something, you typically try to answer the question "what's in it for me?" before they ask it.

The same is true when you ask your customers for a referral. Incentive-based referral strategies work wonders, and can easily be implemented as part of a customer loyalty program, or as part of your existing customer relations systems.

Consider offering customers who successfully refer clients to you discounts on products, free products or services, or gifts. Offer incentives relative to the number of referrals, or the success rate of each referral.

This can have a spin off effect, as your referral customers may become motivated to continue the referral chain. They too will be interested in the incentives you have provided, and tell their friends about your business.

Be Proactive

The only way your referral program will work is if you put some effort into it, and maintain some level of ongoing effort.

Here are some ideas:

- Put a referral card or coupon in every shopping bag that leaves your store
- Promote gift certificates during peak seasons
- Offer free information seminars to existing customers, and ask them to bring a friend
- Host a closed-door sale for your top 20 customers and their friends

Provide Great Customer Service

An easy way to encourage referral business is to treat every potential customer with exemplary customer service. Since the art of customer service is lost is many communities, people are often impressed by simple added touches and conveniences. That alone will encourage them to refer your business to their network.

Stay in Touch

Make sure you are staying in touch with all of your potential and converted customers. Through newsletters, direct mail, or the Internet, keep your business name at the top of the minds, ahead of the competition.

Even if they have already purchased from you, and may not need to purchase for some time, a newsletter or email can be a simple reminder that your business is out there. If someone in their network is looking for the product or service, it will be more likely that your customer will refer your business over the competition.

8

Profits and Leads through Host Beneficiary Relationships

Did you know that a business just down the street from yours may be able to help double your profits this year? Or does this sound a little too far-fetched?

Maybe. If you operate a retail store that sells tires, and the business down the road is a hair salon, you may have a hard time making this happen. However, loose partnerships between complementary, non-competing businesses can be a financial goldmine when implemented strategically. And your partner may be just steps away!

Formally called Host Beneficiary Relationships, these partnerships help small and medium-sized businesses tap into very specific target markets and close sales under existing relationships of trust.

HB Relationships allow one business (the 'host') to add value to their product or service, and the other (the 'beneficiary') to benefit from the impact of a referral. The beauty of this arrangement is that the roles can then be swapped; the 'host' becomes the 'beneficiary' and vice versa.

Like any marketing strategy, HB Relationships don't work for every business all the time. However, they are a great tool to keep in your marketing arsenal when starting a business, entering new markets, boosting product sales, or any other opportunity that requires a specific and personal approach.

How Can a HB Relationship Help Your Business?

Establishing, planning, and implementing a successful HB Relationship campaign is more complex than asking your neighbor to send a letter to his client base with an offer from your company.

As with every other component of your marketing strategy and materials, an HB Relationship campaign must be purpose-driven and evaluated to be the best approach to secure your desired results.

For example, if your business caters to a broad audience and you have an irresistible offer that is going to have people running through your doors, you may want to consider a simple advertisement that will reach the most people. Alternately, if you offer a common product with a low price point – like coffee or candy – it's unlikely that a HB Relationship is worth the cost and effort involved.

So in what cases will a Host Beneficiary Relationship benefit your business?

1. A Start-up Company

A company that is just starting out has the most to gain from a HB Relationship. Faced with the standard challenges of establishing a new operation – credibility, product positioning, target market establishment, marketing strategy, etc. – a HB Relationship is an ideal way to get the business off the ground.

Gaining access to a time-crafted list of potential clients in your target market is an impressive benefit. Getting an established business to communicate your offer on your behalf is an almost guaranteed way to establish your own credibility.

However, start-ups often have the least to offer a 'host' company in exchange for being the 'beneficiary'. Trading client lists is not an option in this case. So what's in it for the 'host'?

The host is seen in the eyes of his customers as providing a reward or an exclusive offer for their continued support and loyalty. The host business earns goodwill and has an excuse to contact his database for the cost of a simple mailing.

2. Entering a New Market

An established business venturing into new territory is in a prime position to benefit from a HB Relationship. Whether the business is known or unknown in the community, tapping into a refined target list will ensure that the right people are communicated the benefits of the new business' offering.

In exchange, the host business may benefit from either the beneficiary's client lists in other marketplaces, or the prestige of offering clients an exclusive offer for a new business in town.

Again, this works best when the target market is highly segmented; otherwise, an advertisement would be a faster and more cost effective strategy.

3. A New Product / Service

As with new marketplaces, launching a new product or service may require tapping into a new or more segmented audience to deliver your message. A HB Relationship with the right partner will help to correctly position your offering, and deliver it to an exact audience.

The host business benefits by offering loyal clients the first opportunity to purchase or use the beneficiary business' product or service.

Defining Your Target Market

This is crucial in establishing a HB Relationship – just like it is crucial in every other aspect of your marketing plan. Not knowing and understanding your target market will put you on the fast track to business hardship, and waste time and money in the process.

You can determine your target market – or target market segment – based on the purpose or intention for seeking a HB Relationship. Are you reaching out to a new segment of your market? Are you offering a new product or service that may appeal to a specific segment of your market?

Are you moving to a new market area and looking to establish yourself amongst your broader target?

Determine your audience and write your target market here:

_____

_____

_____

Selecting a Host Business

Once you have an idea of who your target market is, you can begin to create a list of target host businesses to approach.

Not every business is going to be interested or willing to engage in this marketing strategy – so doing a little bit of research and positioning your offer is well worth your while. To begin, you will want to draft a long list of all potential host businesses.

Do this by considering all business types that would be complementary to – but not competing with – your business.

Those businesses that offer a service or product that is connected in some way to your own. For example, if you operate a hair salon, some potential HB partners would include esthetics salons, clothing stores, drug stores, and perhaps some specialty goods stores.

Or, if you operate a retail tire store, you might consider a list that includes hardware stores, automotive part shops, car washes, auto body shops, or specialty auto part distributors.

Pick up the yellow pages, or conduct a Google search for all businesses in your market area that fall under the categories you identified. You may also consider asking your colleagues and associates for ideas and recommendations.

When creating this list, make sure each business falls under these criteria:

Non-competitive. Their offer should be complementary to, but not compete with, your product or service. Make sure you consider this carefully – seemingly non-competitive offers may actually cannibalize your business.

Remember that your customers have a limited amount of money to spend, and if they begin spending money at your host's business, they might stop spending money at your business.

Same target market. If you and your host business are not talking to the same customer base, then you're wasting your words on customers who are not likely to buy your service or product. If your host business has no idea who their target market is, you may also want to consider looking at other host options.

Start with your customers – your target market or segment of. What services do they use? What products are they interested in? Thinking about their needs will help lead you to the most effective host business.

A killer customer contact list. Without this, they aren't worth approaching – but how do you know they have or maintain a customer database? There are a couple of ways. Pay attention to the type of marketing your potential host conducts. Do they often send letters to their target market? Direct-mail flyers and other promotional materials? Or do they rely on advertising? Do they send a regular newsletter? They also may hold their customer contact information in their point of sale system – if it is technologically advanced enough to do so.

Positive reputation. As the beneficiary, you need to ensure that the host who is referring your business to their customers enjoys a good reputation in the community and with its clientele. Otherwise, you are being endorsed by a business that no one respects, which can be damaging for your reputation.

Host Business Ideas List

Keep track of all potential host businesses using this chart.

Business Name	Contact	Business Type
	Name: Phone:	

	Name: Phone:	
	Name: Phone:	
	Name: Phone:	
	Name: Phone:	
	Name: Phone:	
	Name: Phone:	
	Name: Phone:	

Approaching the Host Business

Once you have created a list of target businesses, it is time to plan your approach. There is some strategy involved in this; you need to convince the host businesses to lend their endorsement and customer contact list to you in exchange for something that will benefit them.

Introduce your product or service. Present your offering to the host business as though you were presenting to your potential customers:

heavy on benefits, and light on features. Assume that the host business has placed themselves in the shoes of their customers, and is evaluating whether your product or service is worthwhile for them.

Provide marketing materials and other supporting information like testimonials and market research to establish your credibility, and your understanding of the people you are trying to reach.

Inform and excite. Provide as much information about how the HB Relationship will work, and be sincere in your efforts. Leave room for their thoughts and contributions to ensure that they buy into the process.

Get them excited about the opportunity you've placed in front of them. Use bright examples, and tell a hypothetical story about one of their customers benefiting from your service. Then, bring it back to the benefits that the relationship or partnership will deliver to their business.

Include an incentive. Be clear about the benefits the host can expect to receive. While you will not always be able to offer something tangible, do your best to offer some incentive to the prospective host business.

If you are an established business, offer them reverse access to your customer database after the initial mailing. Or, if you have room in your margin, offer them a piece of the profits you receive from their customers. Whatever it is, make sure you articulate how this particular partnership is worth their while.

Communicate your rationale. Tell the host why you chose to approach them in particular. Do they enjoy a great reputation in the community? Are they a well-known business with a great sense of camaraderie? Compliment them on their business skills and the great relationships they have built with their customers and in the community.

Then, explain how your business can add value to theirs, and allow them to build on the existing relationships with their clients by offering your services.

Reassure. Communicate the benefits of the HB Relationship to the host, and reassure them that there is no risk involved for them. You are not out to take their profits, or place burden on their resources.

Remind them that you are seeking a complementary business relationship, one that benefits both parties.

Craft Your Message

Once you have secured your host partner, put the plan into action as quickly as possible. Offering to write the letter to their customers will not only give you control over the messaging of the offer, but also reduce the time investment required by the host. The process is simplified for them, and happens sooner for you.

- Just like sales letters and other marketing collateral, your HB offer letter should engage the reader and make them feel as though their needs and interests are cared for.

- The letter should position the host as a thoughtful service provider who sought out an offer specifically for the target audience.

- Your offer should be strong and slightly outrageous. Give deep discounts, or free services, exclusively to this target audience.

- Remember to acknowledge the needs and troubles of your reader, and position your product or service as the answer or solution.

- Include an incentive to act quickly. Ensure your offer is time-sensitive or of limited quantity.

Five Simple Steps to Creating an HB Relationship

In summary, here are is a five-step roadmap to creating a positive, profit-filled, HB Relationship:

- Identify your target market.
- Identify target host businesses.
- Create a unique offer for each host business.
- Approach the host business.

Draft your letter.

Points to Remember

- **Make mistakes in small batches.** If you are unsure about the accuracy of your target market – do a test run. Send a small batch of 50-100 letters to a small group of people, and measure the response.

  o Alternately, you can send three different letters to each third of your target market, and evaluate which offer is acted on the most. This is of benefit for both the host and the beneficiary business because the response rate of the target market is tested, as are their purchase motivations.

- **Create benefit for the host business.** Remember that there must be an incentive for the host business, or the partnership is not worth the time investment. It is important to consider this, and plan ahead before you approach the host business. Create a number of options for the host to choose from, whether it is using your database after the initial mailing, or sharing a piece of the profits.

- **Be honest.** If you are working with several businesses in your area on different offers, make sure each business knows and is comfortable with the arrangement. Ensure that each offer is distinctive and each host is benefiting from the arrangement without competing with other host businesses. This is just good business form.

- **Rest on the strength of your offer.** With a strong offer, your HB campaign will be on the path to success. Make it something your audience can't refuse. Your offer should not only be enticing and engaging for your audience, but should also benefit the host in reputation. Their customers should feel valued and appreciative toward the host for bringing your offer forward.

- **Repeat.** Once you've established one successful HB partnership, keep going! This technique is a valuable way to promote your business and your unique products and services, and can be repeated several times each year with several different host businesses.

Host Beneficiary Letter Template

[Headline in bold at the top of the page – strong statement or question] *[Optional sub headline to explain or answer the question/statement]*

Dear [name],

I hope this letter finds you well and enjoying [insert name or description of product or service previously purchased]. Remember, your continued satisfaction with our [product or service] is guaranteed.

I am writing because I have stumbled upon an exclusive new [product or service] that will [describe how the product or service will meet a need or solve a problem].

[Beneficiary business name] is a [describe business type] that [describe business function]. I recently met with the owner, and was able to secure an unbelievable rate for my existing clients. The [product or service]

is *[describe product or service briefly]*. *Customers who have already purchased have said:*
[list testimonials in bullet form]

[describe limited time or quantity], we are pleased to offer you [describe unique offer here]. This is an opportunity you will not find anywhere else, and an offer that will not be available in stores.

I hope you will be able to take advantage of this amazing [product or service].

Sincerely,
[your name]
[company name]
[phone number]

HB Relationship Worksheet

Target Market:	
Potential Host 1: Name: Business Type:	**Unique Offer:**
Host Benefits:	**Date Contacted:**
	☐ Accepted ☐ Follow-up

Notes:

Target Market:

Potential Host 2:	**Unique Offer:**
Name: Business Type:	

Host Benefits:	**Date Contacted:**
	☐ Accepted ☐ Follow-up

Notes:

9

Buying a Business Successfully

This may seem like an odd topic to include in a small business marketing program. Chances are, if you've purchased this program you already have a business you are focused on growing, right?

Exactly. Stick with me. This section is absolutely related to business growth.

Buying a business is not just about purchasing an already established organization, avoiding start-up costs, and focusing on growth. It's about buying *customers*. Whether you're buying your competition or an organization that offers a complementary product or service, the purpose of buying an existing business is to grow your own base of loyal clients.

That said, buying an existing business is not for everyone, or every business owner. It can be a complex process, with no guarantees of a profitable outcome. You may increase your overhead dramatically in the short term, with no guarantee for a dramatic increase in profit in the long term.

There is also no guarantee that you will secure the clients you are after, or be able to transfer every contract. It may not be the best strategy to grow within your industry, or market conditions.

On the other hand, it could be the smartest business decision you've ever made. After all, when the stakes are higher, so are the rewards.

Mergers + Acquisitions

There are two basic ways to use another organization as a vehicle for business growth:

a) **You can *acquire* the organization by purchasing the business outright;** depending on the nature of your agreement, you will purchase their customers, employees, property, etc.

b) **You can *merge* with the organization to create a new business;** depending on the nature of your agreement, you will combine and own half of your customers, employees, property, etc.

Many business owners choose to acquire their target business, and retain control of all business decisions. Alternately, merging with another organization will typically see both business owners in partnership – equally bearing the challenge of joining two companies as one.

As you will see throughout this chapter, the choices involved in business transactions will be entirely dependent on your specific business, and your unique goals and objectives for its growth.

In general, here are some advantages and disadvantages to consider when evaluating how a merger or acquisition may help your business growth.

Mergers + Acquisitions: Advantages
> Addition of new employees and skills > Addition of new knowledge within industry sector > Acquisition of customers within new market segment > Increase in market share > Potential reduction in competition > Potential reduction in costs and expenses (overhead) > Addition of business intelligence, complementary to existing levels > Gain in tangible assets, as well as intangible assets > Potential growth in revenue and market presence > Ability to further develop products or services, and thereby business > Increase in diversification of business, which increases protection from natural fluctuation of market cycles
Mergers + Acquisitions: Challenges
> Impact of new management on existing employees > Impact of old management's exit strategy > Time management and business performance challenges while agreement is being put together > Reputation of new business (positive or negative) > Integration of two staff groups, including management of compensation and bonus structures > Integration of two sets of systems and processes, or choice between sets > Impact of new systems and processes on old/new employees > Speed of relationship building between new staff and existing management > Impact of merger or acquisition on existing customer base

The Acquisition Process

The process of finding and acquiring (or merging with) a new business can be highly time-consuming, but also highly rewarding. The following is a guide to help you find, negotiate with, and acquire an organization that will enhance your existing business.

Finding the Ideal Business

You may have already located an ideal business for purchase. The announcement that that particular business is for sale may have prompted you to consider an acquisition as part of your growth strategy. Or, you may be considering the idea of a merger or acquisition, and not sure which organization would be an ideal target.

Either way, you will need to assess if your target is truly a diamond in the rough, or just a bad egg.

A good target is another business that sells complementary or competing products or services, and for one reason or another is not realizing its true potential in the market. For example, you would consider a business under seemingly poor management, or in need of relocation. Often these floundering businesses will need simple fixes, like relocation, a surge of new investment capital, or implementation of new systems. Depending on the seller's motivations, these businesses can also be acquired at a relatively low cost.

You will want to ensure that you undertake a comprehensive due diligence process (to be discussed in the next section) in order to confirm your assumptions, and to uncover any information that the owner has not volunteered.

Generally speaking, **a bad target** is another business that sells complementary or competing products or services and is performing well. These businesses have a solid customer base, are making a handsome profit, and under solid management. These businesses will likely expect a high sum in an acquisition, and may not see a benefit in a merger.

Seller's motivations

When evaluating potential businesses for sale, take into account the seller's motivations. This will influence the negotiation process, and will also provide insight into the daily operations of the business. If the business in question is in a complementary market to your own, this can also give you a 'heads up' that upward trends could be shifting.

o **Personal**: health, family problems, divorce, finances, retirement

o **Financial**: bankruptcy, no access to capital, profit levels have peaked, increase in operating costs, increase in professional costs (accounting, legal, etc.)

o **Market**: trends declining, increase in competition, technology out of date

○ **Location**: end of lease, high crime area, new non-complementary development, increase in rent

Where do you find businesses on the market?

The answer to this question is a tricky one. Generally, businesses that are good targets won't be listed for sale, which is why the number once source for locating an ideal business is through word of mouth.

1. Word of Mouth. If you're in the market to acquire a new business, let your closest or best-connected colleagues and associates know. Word of mouth is the best way to get in on a potential deal early – before others catch on to your ideal target and create a bidding war. Tap into networking events in related industries, as well as the networks of your accountant, lawyer, and other advisors.

Keep your eyes open and be aware of how your competitors are faring in the marketplace. Some key clues that may indicate internal strife are:

- customer complaints about the competition
- competitor's employees applying at your business for work
- suspiciously low prices
- senior staff leaving the business

2. Brokers. Brokers can be a great help to your business search, especially if you have limited time to invest in the acquisition process. Get a quote for their services up front – they will expect a commission from the transaction. Remember, there are lots of brokers out there, so try to find a referral thought your existing network.

3. Commercial Investment Magazines. These publications are found mostly in major cities, and list businesses for sale that are attached to property. Retail businesses and apartment buildings are the primary type of organization for sale.

4. Trade Publications. These are great resources for businesses that are looking to break into a new industry or marketplace with an acquisition. Their classifieds section will often list businesses for sale.

5. Online. The Internet and online classifieds sites like Craigslist are another great source for business listings, especially if you are looking to acquire a business outside of your region. Be wary of information you exchange online, however. You may wish to set up an initial meeting to ensure the lead you a pursuing is legitimate.

6. Newspapers. Newspapers can be another source for business listings by category, but also include a high number of scams. Again, be wary when investigating these leads.

Your Acquisition Team

Once you have found your ideal target business, certainly before you make contact with them, it is critical that you assemble a team of advisors to help you navigate through the acquisition process.

Many business owners are wary of engaging expert advice due to the cost involved, which can be substantial. However, it is highly preferable to spend money early on to avoid massive financial surprises after you've signed on the dotted line.

It is a good idea to source your accountant and lawyer – if you don't already have one – from business associates that you trust. These people will need to have an intimate understanding of your business, and keep your best interests at the forefront.

Ensure that you have clear scope of work agreements, and understand the fee structure with each member of the acquisition team. Also, since everyone will have to work collaboratively, it's a good idea to have a face-to-face meeting with the entire team to establish relationships early on.

In general terms, your acquisition team's responsibilities will be:

Accountant	Lawyer
Valuation Target business selection Financial rational for selection Financial forecasting Financing Review of target business financials Liaison with legal team	Lead due diligence process Draft and review purchase and sale agreement Draft a review business contracts, including employee contracts All relevant legal processes Review of warranties and indemnities

Due Diligence + Valuation: How much is it really worth?

After you have identified an ideal target business, approached them, and secured their interest in purchase negotiations, the real work begins.

With the assistance of your acquisition teams, you and seller will need to determine the value of the business in question, and arrive at a price based on that value. The process that establishes how much the business is worth is called *valuation*.

The other critical process you will need to begin is the *due diligence process*. This will help you determine whether this is a good acquisition for your business objectives.

Valuation

The process for placing a dollar value on a business is a complex one. There are many different formulas that can be used – depending on the business in question, whether it is service-based or product-based, new or old, etc. – but each of the formulas are impacted by the hard and soft factors described below.

Hard factors are the tangible assets the company owns. This can include property, buildings, inventory, technology and equipment. These items are fairly simple to attach a fixed price to, and are typically included on the company's financial statements.

Soft factors are the intangible assets that can be attributed to the company. This can include goodwill, location, brand name recognition, and intellectual property – including employees. These factors are complex variables in the valuation formula, and can increase the value of the business dramatically.

Generally speaking, intangible assets are worth what they bring into the company and are valued based on their potential earnings.

Due Diligence

Simply put, the onus is on you and your acquisition team to ensure that the information you receive from the seller is honest and accurate. Failing to do so could cost you hundreds of thousands of dollars after the sale – so don't learn the hard way.

While you can assume the seller is doing their best to provide honest and accurate information, the fact remains that they are looking out for their best interests, and not yours. Therefore, it is your responsibility to gather the information you need to property assess the deal before you enter into negotiations.

Your accountant and lawyer will be able to guide you through the due diligence process, and indicate which financial statements, legal documentation, and bylaws need to be reviewed.

You will need to do your own due diligence to validate intangible assets like goodwill, reputation, and brand awareness. Do not hesitate to talk to their customers, vendors, and anyone else who deals with the company on a regular basis.

Again, your acquisition team should be able to ensure you cover your bases when completing your due diligence. Here is a list of questions you'll want to include:

o How accurate are the financials? Are there any factors that could have falsely inflated or deflated the numbers?

o How realistic are the costs of the products or services? Is there enough or too much allocated to the profit margin?

o What is the true value of the business's inventory? Which items in stock can be realistically sold? Which will need to be discounted and moved quickly?

o Are the lead generation numbers accurate? How many customers are actually walking in the doors? Calling in?

o Is there any information that the seller isn't volunteering that could impact the vitality of the business?

Negotiations

Once you have completed a thorough due diligence and valuation process, the next step is negotiations. You and the seller may have agreed on a loose price for the business, but you still have many other issues to discuss and ultimately cement in a contract form.

A key element to be aware of during the negotiation process is intangible assets. These assets can significantly increase the price of the business during the valuation period, so what guarantees will be implemented to ensure those assets continue to earn at the same level?

Here are some other thoughts to keep in mind when negotiating with the seller:

Be prepared to walk away. Establish a maximum dollar figure you are prepared to spend on the business, and stick to it.

Don't get emotionally involved. Remember that this is a business transaction that may or may not work out. Once your heart or emotional self is attached the deal, it's easy to spend too much, or give up too much.

Establish a continuous flow of communication. Make a strong effort to keep communication flowing throughout the negotiation process. Avoid using your lawyer to pass on negative or confrontational messages. Stay calm, and stick to fact-based negotiation.

Focus on intangible assets. As mentioned above, these assets can quickly inflate the value of a business, and give the seller certain tax benefits. Make sure that every intangible asset is accurately measured and can be reasonably guaranteed to perform after the seller is out of the picture.

Purchase Agreement

The purchase agreement – or buy-sell agreement – puts the agreed-to price and purchase terms in formal, legal contract format. It is important to remember that this is often the only contract, so you will want to ensure it encompasses every possible scenario to protect your interest. Your legal team will be responsible for drafting and reviewing this.

This document will look different depending on the type of business, and the unique considerations that pertain to the terms of the sale. For example, if you are purchasing assets or shares in company, the structure of the legal documentation will be dramatically different.

Here are some elements that you should be aware of:

Warranties. These are essential elements of the purchase agreement. Warranty clauses confirm facts about the business as represented by the seller. These can include assets, liabilities, employees, legal claims, creditors, debtors, and year-end accounts. For example, a warranty clause could state that all outstanding bills have been paid.

Indemnities. Indemnity clauses ensure the seller will pay for unforeseen liabilities related to the business prior to the sale. These could include potential lawsuits, and other costs related to the management of the company before you acquired it.

Overlap period. You may wish to include a clause that will allow you to work in the business for a period of time before the final close. This would give you an opportunity to identify any major issues that would affect the sale, before the deal is sealed. A bailout clause would accompany the overlap period.

Other contracts. Be aware of other contracts the company you are purchasing is engaged in – including employment agreements, leases, and licenses. You will need to be aware of and review these contracts before you sign the final agreement.

Non-compete clause. This will prevent the seller from establishing a competitive business in the same local area or market. If you a buying a consultancy – where the majority of the value of the business is goodwill – you will want to ensure the non-compete clause is present.

Employees + Customers

After you've signed on the dotted line, you can turn your focus to growing the business! The new business's existing employees and customers are two groups of important stakeholders that you will need to communicate, build a relationship, and establish rapport with.

Customer retention

If you have just purchased a new business to expand your own, chances are your new customer base is of high value to you. In most cases, these customers will have an existing relationship with the previous business owner, and may not be willing or excited to deal with new management. I suggest you spend time getting to know your new clients, and working to establish new relationships and confidence in the new management team. Remember that you will lose some clients, but with effective communication and patience, you will retain the best ones.

Staff retention

Business purchase and sale can create much unnecessary strife for staff members. Without fluid communication, the rumor mill takes over and supercharges feelings of uncertainty, change and threats to employment. These things can be damaging to your ability to be an effective manager, so take the time to communicate openly with staff at every opportunity, and involve them in key decision making to earn their buy-in to the process.

Combining policies and systems

Depending on the integration level of the two businesses (old and new) you will want to establish some consistency in the policies and systems of each business. At the very least, you will want to ensure the financial accounting systems are synchronized and systemized to facilitate efficient reporting. At the staff and customer level, ensure that all changes (add, remove or change systems) are clearly discussed, and opportunities for feedback are given. Remember that these changes won't happen overnight, so be patient!

10

Leverage From Marketing Case Studies

The strategies in this program mean absolutely nothing unless you choose to implement them.

The beauty of each of these time-tested strategies is that you can begin implementing them at any time – and start virtually anywhere in the program. There is no need to completely rework your entire marketing campaign or put off making changes until you can make all the changes at once.

This section profiles the success of others who have taken the information in this program and used it to better their businesses.

In each case, it took only a handful of changes to dramatically increase sales and generate higher revenues.

Let their stories motivate you to start working today to better your own business.

Case Study One

Think Coffee News

Business Type: Small Magazine Publisher

Objective: Increase profits with cross selling opportunities, without any time expense.

Strategy: Education

Solution(s): A prominent marketing personality was asked to write a regular column and create a series of workshops. The column and workshops were designed to educate clients on easy-to-implement and cutting-edge marketing initiatives, as well as sell clients a twelve-month program (Starter Program).

Value Add Proposition: The twelve-month program would assist advertising clients on marketing their own business, creating better offers, back end sales, as well as profitable joint-venture opportunities.

Method: Free Series of Marketing Workshops + Newsletter Column

Marketing Materials:
- Sales Script to promote Starter Program
- Email template
- Workshop invitation

Result! A sustainable joint venture and cross selling opportunity was established, and is now worth thousands of dollars in additional revenue per year.

Case Study Two

Young Realtor of the Year

Business Type: Independent Contractor

Issue: Need to increase revenues, but has no extra time available after a successful marketing campaign.

Strategy: Intellectual Capital

Solution(s): When other local realtors phone for free advice, he sells them on shadowing him in action for a day. Less successful realtors ride his coattails for a day and are free to take as many notes as they like. Must guarantee they will not impede his ability to work nor talk to his clients at any stage.

Value Added Proposition: A one-hour debrief is included in the session, plus a hand out to ensure the client experienced/noticed most important parts of day. A less successful realtor is educated, and the young realtor is positioned as an expert through this mentorship program.

Method: Regular, time-consuming phone calls were turned into a source of revenue.

Marketing Materials:
- Sales Script
- Referral Program

Result! Realtor now makes $1,000 per day in addition to successful sales revenues with limited time investment.

Case Study Three

Personal Trainer

Business Type: Independent Contractor

Objective: Need to generate more new leads and create a loyal (more valuable) client base

Strategy: Risk Reversal and Service Packaging

Solution(s): The personal trainer needed to understand why first-time buyers are reluctant to purchase training services. In response, the first session was offered for free to clients who were qualified through a series of questions. This demonstrated credibility, empathy, insight, and most importantly the ability to provide a benefit to the person. Potential clients had the opportunity to evaluate the service before they opened their wallets.

Value Added Proposition: First session free, with package program of services available for $3,000 for Platinum clients.

Method: Advertise and promote free session

Marketing Materials:
- Training Program
- Sales Scripts
- Referral Program

Result! Personal Trainer tripled industry average revenues with this service package that sold for 10 times the industry average.

Case Study Four

Oil and Gas Company

Business Type: Large-format company

Objective: Need to find a way to keep customers coming back; most customers make 'one-time' purchases of large products that sell for approximately $70,000.

Strategy: Maintenance Program (Service Plan)

Solution(s): Machines sold for $70K and seldom had any issues inside five years. A warranty and Maintenance Program was developed to upsell each client, and provide an opportunity to 'get in the door' of the customer. A condition of the warranty is that we must come in quarterly to service the machine and ensure it was in good health.

Value Added Proposition: The $2,500 maintenance program was up-sold to each customer, providing an (almost) unconditional warranty and ease of mind.

Method: The serviceperson who made quarterly visits to each client also served as a salesperson that would look for other opportunities to provide the client with products or services.

Marketing Materials:
- Collateral for other products
- Sales Script
- Questionnaire

Result! The 'lifetime value' of each client went up dramatically, and most sales were increased by $2,500 for the Maintenance Program.

Case Study Five

Accounting Company

Business Type: Service-based Company

Objective: Need to grow business and increase revenues.

Strategy: Education and Expertise Positioning

Solution(s): Educate the market regarding tax strategies 'The Government Didn't Want You to Know'. Position the business as the experts with cutting edge advice and innovative money saving solutions for clients.

Value Added Proposition: Potential clients were able to gain 'free' information from the business, without making a purchase, which eliminates the risk involved in finding an accountant.

Method: Accountant wrote educational and informative tax columns as well as developed a regular string of seminars.

Marketing Materials:
- Newspaper + Newsletter Columns
- Free Seminars
- Referral Program.

Result! Firmly established themselves as the 'go to' company for businesses looking to pay less tax.

Case Study Six

Music Teacher

Business Type: Independent Contractor

Objective: Need to generate more income to support ambitious business owner

Strategy: Risk Reversal + Education

Solution(s): Developed a free Loss Leader two-hour group lesson for adults. The most popular song requested was taught, and all participants were guaranteed to be able to play it after the two hours. His clients (adults) were not interested in playing technically well, just in knowing a few songs to play at Christmas, etc.

Value Added Proposition: Clients were not required to put down any money up front, and would have the opportunity to purchase a 12-month training course to continue to develop their skills.

Method: Loss Leader was heavily promoted, and at the end of the session the students were sold a 12-month training course (highly systemized and very little 'time' attached).

Marketing Materials:
- SWOT Analysis
- Advertisements
- Newsletter
- Joint Ventures
- Loss Leader

Result! Licensed his program. He reckons he will have made more money off 'Unchained Melody' than the Righteous Brothers!

Case Study Seven

Lawn Mowing Business

Business Type: Service-based Business

Objective: Find a way to increase revenues and reduce overhead.

Strategy: Competitor Research

Solution(s): Researched the five most successful businesses in their industry. Found the major competitors were companies selling 'licenses' rather than other lawn mowing companies. Created framework of everything needed to 'license'.

Value Added Proposition: Offer $30,000.00 licenses, rather than $50 lawn mowing jobs.

Method: Took everything the company was doing successfully to operate a 'lawn mowing business', and completed manuals for operations and marketing based on existing systems.

Marketing Materials:
- Operations Manual
- Marketing Manuals

Result! Licensed company and tripled previous year's sales with equal or reduced overhead. PLUS: Realized everything that worked for the lawn mowing business could also work with minor changes for dog groomers and carpet cleaners. Also licensed these businesses.

Case Study Eight

Community Supermarket

Business Type: Product-based Business

Issue: Needs to find a way to compete with other, larger, grocery stores and stop losing money.

Strategy: Joint Venture Marketing

Solution(s): Create a private label alternative with excellent branding and POS (point of sale) material. Joint venture with other small town supermarkets and ensured long term strategy to 'compete with big boys'.

Value Added Proposition: Huge increases in profit margin for an excellent product

Method: Full blown brand strategy.

Marketing Materials:
- Direct Mail
- Newspaper Ads
- Joint Ventures

Result! 22% increase in profitability.

Case Study Nine

Local Restaurant

Business Type: Service-based Business

Issue: Revenues in a downward spiral.

Strategy: Target Market Research

Solution(s): Restaurant found that their clientele had changed, but they were still modeling their business on what had worked in the past. The name was changed from 'Family Restaurant' to 'Pastaria'; younger staff were recruited; a calendar of events was created to draw crowds; and the brand identity was updated. The new image was one that their desired clientele would resonate with.

Value Added Proposition: Past influential customers were invited to try the revamped restaurant for free (through gift certificates).

Method: Personal letters were mailed to all popular and influential people in the local area (athletes, successful business people, Mayor, Council Representatives, Newspaper publisher, etc.).

Marketing Materials:
- Personal Letters including Gift Certificates
- Calendar of Events
- New brand identity

Result! Revenues tripled over twelve months.

Case Study Ten

Business Incubator

Business Type: Service-based Business

Objective: Increase occupancy in short-term offices and increase profit.

Strategy: Risk Reversal; Powerful Offer

Solution(s): A powerful offer was created and targeted at small to medium sized business owners currently operating from home. The offer included minimal financial investment, ease of transition, and no commitment.

Value Added Proposition: New clients were offered their first month free, no deposit, no contract, and a free moving service. There was no risk involved for the client, and a powerful business operation environment was provided.

Method: Direct mail sales letter to potential business clients who currently operate at home, with follow up calls made by contract salespeople to close the sales.

Marketing Materials:
- Sales Letter
- Sale Script
- Referral Program.

Result! Doubled profits in first year and sustained growth..

Case Study Eleven

Business Incubator

Business Type: Service-based Business

Objective: Business Incubator had developed a system that increased occupancy 22% above industry average (this basically doubled 'profits') and needed to find new ways to grow the business.

Strategy: Purchase Competitors

Solution(s): Developed a list of competitors, and created a financial strategy to acquire them. Most of the business centers jumped at the chance to exit the business as they were operating at industry average. Grew business and market share immediately and also created a viable option for someone looking to sell.

Value Added Proposition: The clients received superior service and were provided with greater leverage through the expanded service centers.

Method: Direct mail piece to all business centers offering to purchase.

Marketing Materials:
- Sales Letter
- Sales Script
- Sales Presentation

Result! Bought several of their competitors, increased market share and brand awareness substantially, profits grew by 75%.

Case Study Twelve

Mortgage Broker

Business Type: Independent Contractor

Objective: Talented Mortgage Broker needs to grow clientele

Strategy: Expert Positioning

Solution(s): Increased her fees. Developed series of ongoing seminars, free information conferences, and wrote a column for magazines (hired ghost writer and licensed those available on the net).

Value Added Proposition: People wanted to work with her and seek her counsel because they were able to hear her opinions, numbers, success stories and advice prior to committing.

Method: Public speaking, free information nights and regular seminars/lunch and learns. Systemizing, recording and subsequently scripting initial consultations. She also leveraged existing joint venture with very popular real estate office.

Marketing Materials:
- Phone Script
- SWOT Analysis
- Fax Flyers
- Speakers Notes

Result! $27,245.00 profit in the first month as well as a successful business model that will be able to be licensed/sold.

Case Study Thirteen

Hockey Rink (in Australia!)

Business Type: Service-based Business

Objective: Develop a school league for a sport that was not popular or well known in the Southern Hemisphere.

Strategy: Aggressive Education

Solution(s): Developed a skating program as lead generation and beginner hockey for those interested in trying the new sport. Becoming a school sport was difficult, but the clear and obvious route for immediate and sustainable growth.

Value Added Proposition: Kids and parents were offered an alternative sport activity, and the possibility of being an elite player in a new and emerging league.

Method: Created a school league driven from the ground up through the kids (they spoke to parents... who in turn spoke to the teachers) as opposed to the school system.

Marketing Materials:
- Fundraising Program (for local schools)
- Activities Program (skating, hockey, birthday parties, sleepovers)
- Referral Program (bring a friend)

Result! A school league with over 70 (paid) teams registered and state championships.

Case Study Fourteen

Magician

Business Type: Independent Contractor

Objective: Make a profit!

Strategy: Value Added Packaging

Solution(s): A merchandise program was established to supplement the income generated from regular magic shows. Instead of relying on donations at the end of each show (like most street performers), a table was created with t-shirts and magic kits available for purchase. A salesperson was hired to man the table while the magician worked the crowd.

Value Added Proposition: Instead of a $5 donation, parents and kids could purchase $25 kits for home magic trick practice – a far better value.

Method: Table set up to sell magic kits and merchandise; salesperson was hired.

Marketing Materials:
- POS (point of sale) Material
- Magic Kits
- Uniforms + T-Shirts
- Referral Program
- Sales Training

Result! Tripled income immediately and was referred to larger paid gigs by audience members.

Case Study Fifteen

Magazine Publisher

Business Type: Independent Contractor

Objective: Find a niche market used for publishing expertise. The successful magazine publisher sold her business with a 'non-compete' clause for a high profit. She wanted to continue working and this is the only business she knew.

Strategy: Education + Expert Positioning

Solution(s): Become a consultant. Train other struggling publishing businesses how to turn a handsome profit and avoid the common pitfalls of the business.

Value Added Proposition: Publishing businesses benefit from the expertise of a former competitor, without the high salary. The highly profit but high failure industry of publishing has access to a proven success.

Method: Sales letter followed by a phone call to all local publishing businesses.

Marketing Materials:
- Sales Script
- Sales Letter
- Referral Program

Result! She made more in this business than she did in the last!

Case Study Sixteen

Carpet Cleaning Company

Business Type: Service-based Business

Objective: Need to increase repeat clients and reduce expense of attracting new clients.

Strategy: Client Education + Service Program

Solution(s): Most repeat clients only have their carpets cleaned every three to five years. A customer education program was created to encourage clients to increase that frequency to every six months. With hot extraction steam, the ongoing carpet cleaning program would provide health benefit for clients rather than a health detriment.

Value Added Proposition: The six-month frequency would provide clients with a health benefit, instead of a health detriment.

Method: Educate sales team and train all staff on new scripts, then create marketing material to back up claims.

Marketing Materials:
- Staff Sales Script
- Bonus Structure for Salespeople
- Marketing Collateral

Result! 27% (consistent with standard upselling statistics) of the clients bought into the program resulting in a HUGE increase in profitability.

So What Do You Do From Here?

Now that you have come to the end of this book you have just been given key strategies to use to start growing your business today. These keys have the potential to change your business in a significant way. But that's the thing about keys. Keys only contain potential. Keys alone, like these ideas, will not transform you or your business. They must be put to use.

You have a choice today. You have just collected these master keys and added them to your intellectual collection. You must decide if you will just carry them on the key chain of your mind, jingling around, making noise in your head saying, "Oh, I know that." Or you can do what a key is designed for. You can utilize them. The right key used in the right way can unlock doors of opportunity that have been closed to you to this point. Using the keys you have learned in this book can open you up to realms of profitability and impact that had previously been out of reach without them. But you are without them no longer. These keys are in your possession. They belong to you and can never be taken away. Will you tuck them away in the recesses of your mind or will you put them to work and unlock the treasure that has been in your business this whole time – *Hidden in Plain Sight.*

The choice is yours my friend. Choose wisely!

www.ingramcontent.com/pod-product-compliance
Lightning Source LLC
Chambersburg PA
CBHW071317220526

45468CB00001B/401